W9-AGO-180

HOW TO MAKE
WINE
IN YOUR OWN
KITCHEN

Mettja C. Roate

MB

A MACFADDEN BOOK

To Reggie and Jim,

who supplied patience by the bushel

A MACFADDEN BOOK

First printing.............July, 1963
Second printing...........May, 1966
Third printing..........August, 1967

THIS IS A MACFADDEN ORIGINAL
NEVER BEFORE PUBLISHED IN BOOK FORM

MACFADDEN BOOKS are published by
MACFADDEN-BARTELL CORPORATION
A subsidiary of Bartell Media Corporation
205 East 42nd Street, New York, New York 10017

Copyright, ©, 1963, by Macfadden-Bartell Corporation. All rights
reserved. Published by arrangement with the author. Printed in
the U.S.A.

CONTENTS

CHAPTER I

So You're Going to Make Wine

Congratulations! You are on the threshold of a wonderful new adventure. Awaiting you are new taste thrills, a grand feeling of pride, and an opportunity to observe Mother Nature perform a minor miracle.

There was a time in this land of ours when every household boasted a crock of the family's favorite wine. This was even before prohibition. Then, somewhere along the line, the art and habit of making wine at home was lost almost completely.

With the advent of World War II, the labor shortage forced on us a new do-it-yourself era. People relearned the skills of making their own breads and cakes, sewing at home and even making good butter in a fruit jar. Making wine in your own kitchen is another revival of an old, old culinary art.

Homemade wines will differ from those on the commercial market. First of all, a lot of ingredients that are not used commercially go into them. And the commercial maker would never tackle wine from flowers and fruits and vegetables because of the labor problem and the care required.

Trying to compare homemade wine with the commercial product is like saying that bakery-made cakes, resplendent in their snug cellophane wrappers, are superior to those turned out in the family kitchen, made with good rich butter and whole fresh eggs.

On the other hand, a Moselle, vintage 1937, or perchance a Red Bordeaux, vintage 1928, is to home winemaking as Cordon Bleu cookery is to three square meals a day.

Too, judges of fine wines who overgenerously air, but not necessarily share, their knowledge seldom admit the homemade product on any but a folksy level—like country cooking to the self-conscious gourmet. They are condescending if not rudely critical of the whole idea of homemade wines.

We have an acquaintance who is one of these "judges." For several years he sneered at my winemaking activities and lec-

7

tured me about "false wines." (Meaning, I assume, any wine not derived from the fermented grape.)

Well, one evening when I knew he was coming, I poured the contents of a bottle of Rhine wine, vintage 1927, which my uncle had brought from Europe as a birthday gift for me, into a decanter and put it in plain sight. When the "judge" got around to his subject, the inferiority of home-made wines, I was ready for him. I took my precious birthday gift and carefully poured him a glass, explaining that it was homemade potato wine. (Incidentally, the Potato Wine recipe on page 134 is a close match for a good Rhine wine.)

Hmmm, said he, he could taste a bitterness; he could detect a musty aftertaste, too—must have developed from a good crop of penicillium mold. Why, he could even see by the lack of clarity that this was false alcohol. I smirked, but hung onto my will power and my tongue. My husband, who was equally silent, did not know of my trick until he helped proofread these pages. So, you see, offering homemade wine to "judges" can be pearl tossing.

In writing this first chapter, I feel as if I must help build a mental "crash chamber" for any readers who are going to follow in my winemaking footsteps. For any home wine-maker sooner or later runs headlong into a lot of extremely critical people, often those who are too lazy ever to try any-thing on their own. If they can't buy it in a store, it isn't worth having. Also among the people who consider home wine-making an absurdity are those who say, "Making wine? Huh, I've never been *that* hard up," as if the whole thing were a dipsomaniac's false economy. However, consider the prac-tical facts: By making your own wine, you have a variety and choice that few households could afford, even if such wines were commercially available.

And it is economically sound, too. Making your own wine will supply gallons instead of only bottles, and the variety will be infinite. The cost can be measured in quarters instead of dollars. In exchange for this touch of luxury, you are going to find yourself leaping out of bed like a scullery slave, dash-ing down to the kitchen to stir the mash because you hap-pen to forget it until the middle of the night.

Franklin said, "Time is money." The major expense in homemade wine is purely a matter of time and patience. On the other hand, remember that our hospitals are filled with people who never learned how to do things with their hands and their spare time. Making wine is a wonderful adult hobby. You will have a fifth-row-center seat to watch Mother Nature star in that great production of hers, the Miracle of Fermentation. But more about that later.

Warning also should be issued of the character who should stick to straight Bourbon. He'll sample your wine (by the gallon) and say, "Hmm . . . tastes good, but it doesn't have much of a wallop." For homemade wines seldom jolt you off your feet. Under the natural conditions of fermentation, the highest alcoholic content attained is 12% to 13%. This percentage is pretty average in all commercial unfortified wines, too. The next time you buy a bottle of wine, read the fine print on the label. About 90% of the commercial wines are fortified up to 20% by volume. This literally means that they have been "spiked" with distilled alcohol. Homemade wine with a real wallop can easily be accomplished by fortifying your own product with any good grade of domestic brandy.

The health benefits of wine have long been recognized. It aids digestion wonderfully. It is a relaxing beverage. It warms guests and sweetens tempers. Serving the proper wine with meals makes people show all the good things that they are. Here in America, too many families eat at home as if they were perched on a stool at the corner drugstore. We need to relax at our meals to assimilate the good from the food we have eaten.

The true meaning of the word "wine" is "the fermented juice of the grape." In this book we are going to deal with grapes, too, but most of the recipes are of the "peasant wine" variety. For centuries people have been making excellent wines from things other than grapes. Here again the wine "judge," the purist, may insist upon the dictionary definition of wine, i.e., the fermented juice of the grape. But there are thousands of people who disagree and who have been disagreeing heartily down through the ages.

Making wine from other fruits and grains goes back far into time. During Cicero's tenure of power in Rome, there was a law that prohibited the raising of grapes beyond the Alps. All of the land north of the Alps was for grain fields, and grain fields alone. After all, Rome's breadbasket had to be kept well filled. But the wine-loving farmers got around that. As early as 60 B.C. it is recorded that wine was made from grain and fruit other than grapes.

People have been making wine from other plants ever since. Hungary, with its plum orchards, is famous for its plum wine and for its sliwowitz. The latter is distilled plum brandy, and is practically the national drink in all the Balkans. The Scandanavian countries with their peaches, pears, apples, berries and grains have long made wines and liquors from them.

The old rule of supply seems to govern the winemaking habits of a country; wherever any fruit grows in great abundance, the people soon invent wonderful recipes for wine. Our own colonists made cider from the prevalent apple, let it ferment into hard cider, and then distilled it into applejack. They also made wines from the wild berries they found. Around Mount Vernon the scuppernong grape grew both wild and under cultivation; George Washington made excellent wine from the scuppernong—and, what's more, he sold it!

Making wine is easy, especially if you do it in your own kitchen, a gallon at a time. My husband was deeply bitten by the winemaking bug several years ago, and to this day we have a basement full of crocks big enough to take a bath in, plus innumerable barrels. He has a collection of wine presses, grape crushers, funnels as big as French horns, and at least one of every gadget ever made for winemakers. He gets very perturbed when I insist I want just one gallon of a particular kind of wine. We have two separate winemaking establishments: his (basement) and mine (kitchen). He turns out quantity, and I do what he calls "puttering."

This is all leading up to the fact that this book is aimed at the housewife and her kitchen, whether it be a 12 by 15 room or a Pullman galley three steps wide. Delicious wine can be made right where the daily cooking is done, without any investment in expensive equipment. In the following chapter I am going to list the items needed, which are probably all on hand right now.

Before making wine, there is just one thing to remember: A winemaker's permit is needed. It doesn't cost a cent, and is usually obtainable in the same government office where income tax is paid. Simply ask for United States Treasury Department Internal Revenue Form #1541, which is titled "Tax Free Wine for Family Use."

The only limitation made by the government is the amount of wine permissable to make. Upon the filing of Form #1541 permission is granted to make two hundred

(200) gallons of tax-free wine. That is a lot of wine. Picture 200 gallon jugs in a pyramid! Or better yet, multiply by four quarts, and picture 800 wine bottles in a pyramid. That is really a lot.

Form #1541 requires full name and address, where the wine will be produced and stored, marital status, whether you are the head of a family or are single, and whether or not you have dependents living with you.

You are also required to sign a promise not to sell the wine you produce, and not to make it in partnership with other persons. Partnerships come into a different category with regard to Federal regulations for winemaking. You must also pledge not to make wine for a person who is not a member of your family. Form #1541 has to be made out in duplicate before one drop of winemaking is begun. Send both copies to the local district supervisor of the Alcohol and Tobacco Tax Division for examination. When it has met his approval, it is stamped and the carbon copy is returned to you to be posted or kept where the wine is to be made. When the approved copy of Form #1541 is received you are ready—but not a minute before!

This is not a lifetime permit, by the way, but must be renewed every year. The year is reckoned as beginning on July 1 and ending on June 30.

CHAPTER II

The Equipment Is in Your Kitchen

Now that U. S. Internal Revenue Form #1541 is filled out and in the mail, start taking inventory of what is on hand that can be used for wine making. If you cook three meals a day and perhaps do a little canning in summer, most likely nothing will have to be bought. The following items are listed in order of use in a typical wine recipe:

1. *A Two-Gallon Container*

Traditionally, wine and crocks go together. If you have fallen heir to a two-gallon gray or brown pottery crock, good. The type I mean usually turns up at farm auctions, but often these are cracked, so bid warily. If you feel that you have to follow winemaking tradition, and must have a crock, they are available from any of the mail order houses that cater to farm folk—Sears Roebuck, Montgomery Ward or Spiegel's. The crocks are listed in their catalogues, and are very inexpensive.

But why not join me in throwing tradition to the wind and buy a dual-purpose wine-mash kettle? My favorite dual-purpose kettle is a heavy blue-and-white-speckled enamel-coated canner kettle. It has two handles on the sides for easy carrying, and a loosely fitting cover. It also comes with a fine wire rack which fits the interior snugly and will accommodate seven quarts of canned food for hot-water processing. I have one manufactured by the Federal Enameling and Stamping Company of Pittsburgh. The enamel coating is exceedingly heavy and chip proof.

I like the canner kettle for mash because it is light and easy to handle. The cover keeps dirt out, yet provides enough freedom for the gases to escape from the wine. The cover puts an end, too, to the fuss of tying a cloth over the crock opening, so that it ends up looking like a mummy. Not having to tie and untie the cloth for each stirring of the mash saves a lot of time.

Another alternative to a crock or a canner kettle is two gallon-sized wide-mouthed jars such as are sold wholesale to restaurants for mustard, pickles, and mayonnaise. Most restaurant keepers will give these jars away, as they are non-returnable and end up in the junk pile anyhow. However, working with gallon-sized jars will have disadvantages if you are aiming for a gallon of wine. It means dividing the mash in two, and pouring it from one to the other during fermentation to keep both jars of wine even.

There is still another mash jar which is ideal, but hard to find: the two-gallon clear-glass jar with a wide mouth and a wire handle. It stands about two feet high. This is perfect, offering many advantages over those already described—cleanliness for one thing, and portability for another. But they are very scarce.

If you have read any books on wine lore, you may question my recommending the canner kettle with the hard enamel coating. Most of the books shy away from metal of any kind, even enamel-coated metal. However, such great strides have been made in the coating of metals that this canner kettle has a surface as hard as any pottery-glazed crock you can buy. There is one caution: Do not chip the surface in any manner—especially when stirring the mash. There is always an urge to whack the spoon against the side of the kettle to clean it. Avoid this, and avoid dropping enamelware for fear of chipping off portions along the bottom edge. But with care, the canner kettle is fine.

I firmly believe that avoiding enamelware for winemaking in years past was due to the unperfected product. All sorts of talk about metallic-tasting wine, and wine that would instantly turn to vinegar if it touched any metal, I consider bosh. Probably the old-timers' equipment was not in the cleanest condition in the first place.

2. A Good Sturdy Potato Masher

If you have one of the old-time wooden ones, wonderful! If you have the modern pronged-wire type, this is good, too.

3. A Chopping Blade

A chopping blade will save time and lots of hard work while the wine is fermenting. I have a favorite called the

13

"Foley Chopper." This is a clever three-bladed affair. The two outer blades are stationary; the middle one works up and down with a spring action. This is especially good for apples and vegetables, because it ejects any large pieces and leaves a clean blade for the next downstroke. There is no clogging of fruit which must be pulled out by hand. The Foley Chopper sells for about a dollar and is a good investment for any kitchen. However, if you already have a circular or a two-bladed half-moon-shaped chopping blade, either will do the job well, too.

4. A Large Wooden Bowl

A large wooden chopping bowl, about 10 inches in diameter, or a wooden chopping board about 10 inches square, will make winemaking easier. The bowl is the better of the two because the fruit is confined by the sloping sides. If you do not own a wooden bowl, you can make a three-sided wooden box for chopping. Make the sides about 3 inches deep, and leave one end open for scraping the chopped material into the kettle or crock.

5. A Half Dozen New Paint Paddles

You can beg these paint paddles from the hardware store. These are wonderful for stirring the mash, because their surface is free from grooves and places for bacteria to cling. They have a nice little hole at one end by which to hang them. If they are accidentally dropped into the mash in the stirring process, they rise to the top immediately.

6. A Jelly Bag and Rack

In all of these recipes you will find directions for straining the wine through a jelly bag after the first fermentation. A jelly bag is an absolute necessity. Strainers of the metal variety will not serve the purpose; any that are large enough to hold the mash are too coarsely meshed. If you get one fine enough, it's usually meant for straining tea, and it would take eons to strain a whole gallon of wine. There is a jelly bag and rack on the market for about three dollars which is wonderfully convenient.

If you do not care to spend the money, you can make yourself a strainer out of two broom handles and a ten-pound muslin sugar or flour bag. First of all, carefully examine this bag for holes and, if there are any, mend them very tightly. A strainer with holes in it will obviously not work effectively.

Then lay the bag flat on the table with the open end toward you. Rip the edges of the bag three inches on each side, so you can make a "hem" around the top of the bag. With good strong thread, #20 or store string, reinforce the edges below the rips so the bag will not rip any more, no matter how great the pressure.

Turn back the three inches of material at the top and hem it against the body of the bag, leaving the ends open. (The broom handles will be "threaded" through here, the way a curtain rod goes through the top of a drape.) When making this hem, machine sewing is ideal; but if it has to be sewn by hand, use a close overcast stitch that will not break under strain.

After the broom handles are inserted in the top of the bag, the handles can be placed between two kitchen chairs, with the bag hanging down toward the floor. A crock is then placed on the floor under the bag, ready to catch the juice when you put the mash in the bag.

This homemade strainer has many advantages. In the first place, if you're soaking one bag to remove fruit stains, you can always find another around the house to use in your next winemaking project. In the second place, having the bag propped open by the broom handles leaves both your hands free to load the mash into the bag. When the loading is done, the strainer requires no further attention; the mash can be left to drip under its own power while you are busy with the next winemaking step. The final advantage of this type of strainer is that the broom handles are such sturdy wood they will not bend or break when you twist the bag to extract the last drop of juice.

7. *An Accurate Quart Measure with a Side Handle*

There are many varieties of quart measures on the market, ranging from heatproof pitchers to enameled ones with the gradations printed on the interior. The quart-sized enameled saucepan with the interior markings can also be used by the winemaker. If you have none of these, use a quart milk bottle. But beware of pouring boiling-hot water into a milk bottle; breakage is frequent and dangerous.

8. *An Accurate Measuring Cup*

In measuring cups, the heatproof variety is my favorite. Every household has at least one of these "for free" cups which have been given away over the years with cereals and flour; be careful here, too, of putting boiling-hot water into a measuring cup which is not marked heatproof.

9. *A Plastic Bowl Cover*
(the very largest size)

This is strictly a timesaver if you are using a crock instead of the canner kettle. Measure the diameter of the crock, and either conduct a search for a large enough bowl cover, or buy a plastic tam-o-shanter shower hat. I usually buy the shower hats, because they are made of stronger plastic and have a much longer life than the bowl covers. Too, the elastic edge is wonderfully strong compared to that found on ordinary covers.

Should you not care to invest in the bowl cover or the shower hat, you can use several thicknesses of old bed sheeting, cutting the sheeting three inches larger than the crock and hemming it up with an elastic insert, just as with commercial bowl covers.

10. *A Good Large Funnel*

Be sure your funnel is one that has a little ridge pressed into the side of its beak. Most good funnels have one. In winemaking, the ridge is needed so air can escape from the bottle as the wine takes its place. Checking this small factor will save a lot of wine and aggravation. I recently purchased one made of flexible milky-hued plastic which is excellent for winemaking. It is breakproof and will not transfer flavor or odor from one wine to another. There are no seams to harbor dirt.

11. *Rubber Siphoning Hose*

You will need one 36-inch-long hose with an opening of

one-quarter inch. This can be purchased at any good drugstore. There is one on the market made of red rubber with a squeeze bulb which eliminates having to siphon the wine out by mouth. There is another good variety without the bulb, which is made of beige-colored latex, and is almost transparent. This is helpful because you can see through it in the event that a seed or a piece of fruit is drawn up by accident.

The good old red rubber bathroom variety of hose will serve, too. If there is one on hand, sterilize it by boiling for 20 minutes before using.

12. *Two One-Gallon Clear-Glass Jugs*

Try to get glass jugs that wine has been stored in previously. Avoid using ex-vinegar jugs, for unwittingly you might contaminate the wine with vinegar. Since gallon jugs are difficult to wash with a bottle brush, avoid any that may retain an odor from previous use; it could be detrimental to the wine.

These gallon jugs are used to hold the wine while you are preparing the cheesecloth strainer described in the next paragraph. They come in handy, too, if the canner kettle or crock is needed in the meantime for another batch of wine; during the second fermentation you can store the wine in these jugs without any harm. Wine can also be stored in them for the settling and clearing process. When to settle and clear each particular wine is described in each recipe.

13. *A Cheesecloth Strainer*

A simple and yet convenient cheesecloth strainer can be made from three thicknesses of cheesecloth and a strong piece of cord. I prefer the cheesecloth which comes packaged in sheets of three and is sold at the cleaning-aids counter in most supermarkets. This packaged material is superior to the yard-goods variety, because the edges are bound in a sort of faggot stitch which permits washing and using the cheesecloth over and over again.

The method for straining through cheesecloth can be exceedingly simple, or it can be done the hard way. First of all, draw the wine off without straining; if there is a settled portion at the bottom, avoid this by keeping the hose high

17

enough in the kettle. Once the wine is put into the gallon jugs just mentioned, the settlings at the bottom of the kettle can be put into a separate fruit jar to settle further. Later, you can combine the clear wine which rises to the top with the rest of it. When the wine is out of the crock or canner kettle, scrub the kettle well with scouring powder and rinse with boiling-hot water. This not only kills any bacteria which may be enjoying life up on the sides above the wine level, but it will also warm the receptacle. Putting the wine back into this warmed-up kettle will keep the fermentation at an even rate, in the event that its temperature has dropped while standing in the gallon jugs.

After the kettle is thoroughly cleaned and warmed up, place the three sheets of cheesecloth in layers over the top. Tie in place with a stout cord. I find that making a king-sized rubber band from three inner-tube rubber bands (such as little boys use in their slingshots) works wonderfully well. A good stout piece of notion-counter elastic will also do. Some notion counters carry a corded elastic which is about one-eighth inch in diameter; this is strong and trustworthy, but very hard to find. In putting the cheesecloth over the canner kettle or crock, do not make it drumhead tight, but rather push a dent in the middle of it so there is a place for the wine to form a puddle as it is being strained. After all this, the wine is ready to strain back into the crock or canner kettle for settling before bottling.

14. A Five-Quart Mixing Bowl

A large mixing bowl is a necessity. It should be of crockery, enamel, or stainless steel. There are many recipes in this book which call for one portion of the wine mash to be separated from the remainder of the mash overnight. A large mixing bowl serves wonderfully. It is a perfect piece of equipment, too, while you are preparing the fruit to go into the mash.

15. Bottles for the Wine

Some people collect stamps and coins; you can start collecting bottles immediately. (Not old vinegar bottles, for there is too much danger of vinegar contamination.) The ideal bottles are those which were made for wine in the first place. Usually they have an indented bottom to retain any of the settlings. They are made of rather heavy dark glass, which prevents breakage from pressure and loss of flavor from light. Almost every imported wine is in a brown or green glass bottle. If colored glass bottles aren't handy, use clear glass; but if you do so, be sure to store the wine in a dark cupboard or cellar where light will not get at it. If the wine is to be kept in the back of kitchen cabinets which are opened daily, cover the bottles with several thicknesses of brown wrapping paper.

16. Corks Are Important

You will need corks—real corks made of cork—the old-fashioned push-in kind which will require a corkscrew to extract. Try to locate the exact size cork for the bottles you have collected. Remember that old musty corks can ruin a whole bottle of wine which otherwise might have been delicious. If new corks can't be had, boil the old ones for at least 30 minutes in a covered pan. Cork is a porous material and provides an ideal camping site for germs, odors, and mustiness. I boil my new corks, too, for at least 20 minutes. This not only expands them, but will put an end to any dust and germs which may have jumped in a handy crevice during shipment to get a free ride. Utter cleanliness is the first step to success in winemaking.

You might question why the commercial wine companies ship their wine successfully in screw-type bottles. Well, their wine is not only highly fortified, but pasteurized. Screw caps can only lead to tragedy for the home winemaker, for they have a nasty way of tightening down during fermentation, as any overflow may cause them to corrode. Until a wine bottle has gone up in a blast in the middle of the night, the word "explosion" may be meaningless to you. But we have a ceiling in one part of our basement which has a strange topaz glisten from imbedded glass. We used screw caps on three bottles, because we ran out of corks. Never again!

Old-fashioned push-in corks will never let you down in this manner. The cork may blow out, but it won't take the bottle with it. You may get an occasional wine spray on the ceiling, but this is nothing compared to the danger of splintered glass.

17. *A Pound Block of Paraffin*

You will need one of those pound blocks of paraffin that is put out for the home jelly maker. In the chapter "The Spirit Is Willing If—" complete directions for the final sealing of wine bottles with paraffin are given. Commercial wines are usually sealed with foil or plastic coating, but paraffin does just as well. This is a small investment to make in return for the insurance of having good wine.

18. *A Pair of Plastic or Rubber Gloves*

Owning a pair of "wine gloves" is not a must, but they are good to have if you like to look trim from the cuticle up while in the wine business. In all of the recipes given, stirring the mash with a wooden paddle is recommended. However, there comes the time when you feel that if you could get your hands down into the mash for a good squeezing, it would be much better. For this urge, get a pair of cheap plastic mitts or rubber gloves to be used for wine only; it is easy to carry over an odor of wall cleaner or furniture polish on rubber.

Wine will build up an alcohol volume of 12% to 13%, but in daily doses even this small amount can make the prettiest manicured hand look like a bricklayer's. Used externally, alcohol is a natural solvent of fatty substance; the natural oils of your hands will disappear from constant contact with it.

This sums up the essentials needed to start making wine at home. In listing the items required, I have followed the sequence of use from a typical recipe. Read over the recipes chosen, then gather the materials as they are needed in each step.

CHAPTER III

The Spirit Is Willing If—

Whether you realize it or not, secretly you have been carrying on a process of fermentation from your prenatal days. The human digestive process is a form of fermentation. People who are lifelong teetotalers might get quite a jolt if they really knew that their own stomachs were privately operating a miniature still.

Why fermentation happens is one of the problems which science is still trying to solve. There are books and more books full of theories on the subject. For the home winemaker to equate chemically what he is doing would take another whole lifetime of work, and he wouldn't even get his first mash started. But we know this: Fermentation will take place if plain water and sugar are mixed and kept at an even temperature of 70° F.

Grapes, the darlings of the wine industry, carry the greatest number of wine-yeast cells. The formal technical name for these cells is *Saccharomyces Ellipsoideus.* These cells are present, too, on the skins of almost all ripe fruits which are recommended here for winemaking. Cooperative wasps, bees and other insects are responsible for their distribution. These insects don't always keep their noses clean and sometimes bring into the picture false yeasts and molds. Under the conditions of fermentation, the true yeasts soon sock them silly and take control of the mash. To aid them in holding this power, the home winemaker adds commercial yeast; you will note this in glancing over the recipes.

The great scientist, Buchner, made the biggest strides in the understanding of the creation of alcohol. He discovered that it was the secretion of the yeast cell which caused fermentation. He called this substance *Zymase.* Present-day bacteriologists regard it as an enzyme mixture. The field of enzymes is just being opened up, too, and there may come a day when the home winemaker can buy a little pellet of the proper enzyme solution to produce in a day the same results which now take weeks.

Though fermentation of wine and beer is centuries old as an art, the reasons why it occurs at all remain in the laboratory of the future.

Stages in Home Winemaking

The first time I picked up a book on how to make wines, I, like Omar Khayyam, "came out the same door as in I went." I was just plain baffled by the references to "first" and "second" fermentations.

The first fermentation means that the container of mash is working with the aid of oxygen—the surface of the mash being exposed to air. In other words, it is the period in winemaking when there is no need of an airtight cover. In fact, during this first fermentation great quantities of gas work out of the wine and have to have a wide surface from which to escape. This first fermentation is usually in two parts: First all the elements of the mash are present; then the substance is strained and returned to the same container for a continuation of the fermenting process without the presence of the actual fruit.

The second fermentation is the period within the loosely-capped bottle. In other words, the wine is lightly corked to permit it to throw off the carbon dioxide accumulated. People who cork bottles too tightly during this second fermentation period are the ones who tell tales about wine bottle explosions.

In all of the recipes in this book, I have designated the fermentation periods in simple terms of weeks, so that there is no bewilderment about "first" and "second" fermentation. Make the wine according to these directions, and you will go through first and second fermentation without even knowing it.

How to Keep from Having Wine Worries

A calendar is the prime requisite for peace of mind in winemaking. I like the big ones that some companies give away to their customers. These calendars are about a yard square and have big black numbers that could be easily read from the bottom of a well. If going into production of more than one gallon of wine, get one of these calendars. Tie a string around a pencil and hang it and the calendar in a convenient place.

When the mash is first mixed, mark the date. Then reread the recipe very carefully. If it says put through the jelly bag in two weeks, drop down two weeks on the calendar and put a reminder. If it says that two weeks after the jelly bag performance the wine goes into bottles, put down another reminder.

The best policy is to start the wine on an unbusy night of the week. I always like Fridays because I know that, if I happen to miss a reminder, I have the whole week end to catch up.

Incidentally, that's another subject which worried me when I first started making wine. The books would say, "Let stand fourteen days, no more, no less. . . ." Well, I found myself in a frenzy if I happened to forget until the fifteenth day. Time *is* important in winemaking, but it is not a bit like running a railroad; it is not a split-second affair. If, on the night of the fourteenth day, your youngest decides to drive his new tricycle through the just-paid-for picture window and in the turmoil the wine is forgotten, nothing too serious is going to happen. Just don't get so careless you let the mash go unattended for weeks, or there will be more vinegar around than you can ever use on salads.

This calendar method is the best I've found thus far, outside of using one of these "professional reminder services."

Another handy item for the worry-free winemaker is a good thermometer. This can be a close friend of fermentation. It should be an accurate one, placed near the fermenting wine. Wine is almost human in its temperature range—when fermenting, it is in the seventies and early eighties. If at any time you notice a drop in the temperature, it is wise to cover the wine with several thick pieces of cloth or some heavy material to prevent sudden chilling. A quick rise in temperature is nothing to worry about; just don't put fermenting wine in direct hot sunlight. When the temperature of the mash goes down, the rate of fermentation is slowed up. In relation to this, too, avoid placing the fermenting wine on a cement floor below ground level. If your wine is to be made in the basement, it is good to set the crock or canner kettle up off the floor and away from all drafts.

If you have read any of the recipes before reading this chapter, some of the ingredients which are used to obtain the final delicious product may seem peculiar. But there is a good reason for including them.

Toast is the first one people always question. Well, toast serves two purposes in winemaking. It acts as a wonderful suspension bridge for the yeast, and as a subtle coloring agent. In all cases where toast is used, moistened yeast is spread on in much the same way as bread is buttered. The piece of toast is floated, yeast side down, on the surface of the liquid. This floating suspension gives the yeast cells a chance to continue the growth they started in the yeast factory. It permits the cells to work down slowly through the wine while they are doing their miraculous job of creating alcohol. Any one of the wines that calls for the yeast-and-toast combination could be made without it, but then the period of fermentation would be too long to be worthwhile.

Regarding the coloring ability of toast, you've probably scraped an overdone (*not* burned) piece of toast into a sink where a few drops of water were present. Remember how beautifully brown those water drops became? Well, the same thing happens to wine—the toast acts as a very gentle and subtle coloring agent. Whole-wheat toast will give a deeper amber than white toast, and those recipes definitely calling for whole-wheat toast need the deeper amber coloring. But never use toast which has been burned; it will only add a burnt-toast taste to the wine. To get the right topaz tint in your wines, toast the bread as if it were for breakfast.

Another eyebrow raiser used in home winemaking is shredded wheat or Ralston Purina Company's bite-size Wheat Chex. Either of these will aid in the fermentation process. Using wheat as a fermenting agent is as old as the hills. Some of the "heirloom" recipes in my collection call for a small bag of "stone-ground flour, browned in the oven until the shade of an oak slab." Believe me, using the commercial cereal is much easier. This will also serve to explain why some recipes call for cracked wheat and whole rye—they, too, are good fermenters. Cracked wheat and whole grain rye are obtainable at health food stores. Also, supermarkets carry cracked wheat under several names as a breakfast cereal.

Why There's a Difference in Raisins

A peek ahead at some of the recipes will have indicated quite a bit of fuss about the different kinds of raisins used in the various mashes. Some call for muscat raisins; others call for white raisins. The selection has to do with coloring and flavor. Muscat raisins give a headiness to wine and will add an amber color. White raisins make a "Rhine-ish" flavor and keep a light wine light.

There is no iron-clad rule for these choices; they are the result of personal preference in our own winemaking. If, in a pinch, when the recipe calls for white raisins and you have only the dark on hand, use them. Omitting raisins of some kind at the proper stage may ruin wine. Remember, raisins are grapes in disguise, and their addition at the called-for point in the recipe is very important for successful fermentation and good wine.

Coloring Wine is Ethical

Some wines need no color other than that resulting from fermentation and aging. But the deep reds and bright golds of commercial wines are not necessarily natural beauties. It may come as a surprise to hear that about 70% of commercial wines are artificially colored. This practice is not to be condemned; it's just good salesmanship. The fact that the product is colored should appear on the fine print portion of the labels. If it isn't there, this means that the coloring agent was introduced into the wine during the first fermentation; then it is not necessary to print it on the label. So do not feel the least bit squeamish or unfair about being tempted to make red wine a little redder with red food coloring, or golden wine more golden if it comes out looking weak and insipid despite its wonderful flavor; just add some yellow food coloring. When choosing food colors, be sure they are coloring agents *only*, without any flavoring, such as strong cinnamon or clove.

Serving a highly colored wine is far more impressive than offering one that just hints at the color it should really be. We've all put an artistic sprinkling of paprika over a drab creamed dish to make it look appetizing; so it is with wine. It should have eye appeal, bouquet and taste. After all, our reaction to all food depends on how it looks as well as how it smells and tastes.

There are a lot of factors which will make a wine look less attractive than it should. I've noticed in some very rainy seasons that my Concord Grape Wine did not get as deep in color as it did during a season of many sunny days. In these off years I add several tablespoons of red coloring to the wine just before letting it settle. Putting suitable color in wine is as fair and legitimate as wearing lipstick. If it makes your wine prettier—do it!

The Glycerin Trick

Have you ever been served a glass of wine that seemed to crawl right back up the sides of the glass after you had taken a sip? When that happens in a group of wine samplers, someone usually remarks, "Boy, look at the body this stuff has!"

That body is just an old trick, and one that was passed on to me by a genuine "Kentucky still watcher." All that is needed to get this "stick-to-itive" quality in wine is the addition of an ounce of glycerin per gallon just before the final settling period.

Glycerin is really highly solvent in alcohol; it is very sweet if you put a drop on your tongue. Druggists use glycerin to sweeten many prescriptions and make them more palatable. It will mix readily with wine, and adds only an infinitesimal amount of sweetness to the taste. Glycerin causes wine to cling to the side of the glass in beautiful slow-moving little rivulets.

Commercial winemakers add glycerin to their wines, especially the dark red still wines, as a matter of course. A certain amount of glycerin is always present from the fermentation itself, but often it is not sufficient to give the wine this wanted "coating" ability. Adding glycerin, like adding color, is ethical and just good winemakership.

Clearing Wine

Most wines, if properly made, will clear themselves. However, in some of the rhubarb wines, for example, the recipes call for crushed eggshells. The eggshells act as collection agencies. They draw up all the small solid particles that refuse to lie down by themselves in the heyday of fermentation. (Wine is cleared commercially by an electrostatic method, but obviously the home winemaker cannot do it that way.)

But if one eggshell makes a gallon of wine clear, it's a mistake to think six will make it clearer; too many eggshells will clear it very well—of particles and of all the coloring matter, too.

Isinglass is perhaps the oldest and finest clearing method known in the wine business. However, if you use isinglass, be absolutely sure none of it gets into the wine bottle. Sad to relate, it has been my experience that asking a druggist for a flaked isinglass filter is like asking for a size-14 bustle frame. Chemical houses still use and handle it, but chemical houses are seldom just across the street. Besides, they only sell isinglass in 25-pound lots. Eggshells are a good, cheap, always-handy substitute.

Peppercorns

Perhaps another eyebrow raiser in these recipes is the frequent recommendation for use of eight to ten peppercorns. Well, pepper has no flavor—what we think we taste is a sensation of heat, so the encyclopedias tell us. (I disagree. I believe that home-ground pepper has a definite flavor, compared to that dusty, already-ground stuff in cans. In this case, we are interested in the heat sensation the pepper gives. A glass of wine that starts warming up in the mouth and doesn't stop until it hits the toes has a built-in heater made of peppercorns!

Peppercorns will add heat to any wine without impairing the flavor. Discretion and imagination must be exerted as to which wines should be "heated by pepper" and which should not. I have recommended peppercorns in the wines which are most suited to that warm-inside feeling after they have been drunk.

On the subject of pepper in alcoholic beverages, many years back the father of a friend of mine made a fortune selling "the strongest whiskey in town." His method was simple: When he got in a hogshead of the cheapest whiskey money could buy, he'd dump in a pound of ground pepper and let it settle to the bottom of the barrel. He had the operation down to such a science that the amount of pepper he added never reached above the bung faucet on the barrel. People came from far and wide to buy this extra-warm whiskey at fabulous prices without ever catching on to his secret warmerupper.

Peppercorns rather than ground pepper are recommended for the simple reason that they are easy to strain out. Ground pepper makes the wine so cloudy that you would have no end of grief in clearing it.

Other Flavoring Agents

Some of the recipes are going to call for candied ginger. Ginger root can be used, but I find that the candied ginger has a higher, more refined flavor. Most candy stores handle it. It is expensive by the pound, but never more than a fourth of a pound is needed for a batch of wine.

Cassia buds are called for in many of the recipes, too. These are tiny buds with a high cinnamon flavor. I prefer these to stick cinnamon, because I have found the latter has a tendency to give wine a woody, musty taste.

All Sugar is Sweet, But. . . .

Every housewife knows that if she wants a sparkling glass of jelly, she can bank on pure cane sugar for the best results. For some reason or other, cane sugar produces clearer wine than do the other sweetening agents on the market. Pure honey is the one exception; this is taken up in the chapter "Meads, or Wines Made with Honey."

I may be talking through my new spring hat, but personally I have found more success with cane than with beet sugar. There may be something in the cellular make-up of cane sugar which lends itself better to being made into alcohol than does beet sugar.

Beet sugar will ferment, too, and at the exact rate as cane sugar under similar conditions, but I found that the clearing of wine took longer.

I do not recommend such substitutes as dextrose or maltose when good cane sugar is obtainable.

Using Canned, Dried and Frozen Fruits

In several of the recipes I advise the use of canned fruit. This is usually due to the fact that the flavor combination is made up of two ingredients which are not in season at the same time. Rather than make up two separate wines, and spend a lot of time and effort blending them to get the desired flavor, I just use canned, dried or frozen fruit. This requires only the making of one mash, one aging process. Using canned fruit will in no way impair the fermentation process.

Knowing that canned fruit is packed under high steam conditions would make one think that all the good yeast cells had expired. This is quite true, but the cells from the fresh fruit will soon climb all over the canned fruit and go on working as if canning had never taken place. The same applies to frozen fruit. Freezing kills the yeast cells, but frozen fruit produces excellent wine when used in combination with fresh fruit.

Dried fruit added to wine seems to take up with yeast cells like long-lost buddies at a reunion. The fruit swells up and starts making alcohol, just like that. One might be skeptical about some of the sulphur-drying processes used at present, but to my knowledge this sulphuring of fruit for drying purposes apparently has no effect on the wine. A small amount of oxidation may be set up from it, but so little that it does not matter.

Some Bottling Hints

In the chapter "The Equipment Is in Your Kitchen" I went into the subject of bottles and what they should be. Here I am going to deal with a few tricks which will put better wine in those bottles.

The first (which I have not discovered elsewhere) concerns the use of artists' charcoal sticks. These pieces of charcoal, used in sketching, are about one-quarter inch in diameter and five inches long. They are apparently made from very clear hardwood—the same stuff that a good charred barrel is made of. If you want a keglike flavor to your wine, here's how: Purchase several charcoal sticks and break them up into two-inch pieces. Put one piece into each bottle at the final corking. It will act as a clearing agent, and at the same time will add a flavor that will make the wine taste as if it had spent four years in a keg. The stick of charcoal is easily removed before serving.

If artists' charcoal sticks aren't available, make some out of hardwood dowels. Burn them in the fireplace, furnace, or in the coals the next time there's a weiner roast. Be sure to take them out when they are charcoal and not ashes. Charcoal is just half-burned wood, anyhow. So it is with the liquor industry's highly prized charred barrels. The inner surface of these barrels is saturated with alcohol and then a match is thrown in and the inside is allowed to burn until the alcohol is dissipated. Then an airtight bung-stopper is put in the barrel and the still-smoldering fire dies for want of oxygen.

Cleaning bottles could be a chapter by itself, as there are so many tricks involved. Detergents are wonderful for the purpose. All detergents are designed to make water "wetter." This wetter water will really remove almost anything on glass. Detergents can make grease take a back seat. I never use soap, as we used to know it; in rinsing, the scum is too hard to get rid of. A little overlooked soap scum in a bottle can ruin all the wine in it. Always wash bottles in water as hot as your hands can stand; this is a good step toward cleanliness.

One of the best things to own for cleaning bottles is a good brush. The conventional type are meant for baby bottles and have handles too short for wine bottles, but if you own one of these, you can lengthen the handle with several strands of stout wire. If buying a brush, get one intended for cleaning radiators. Such brushes have very hard nylon bristles, and nice long handles—the ideal winemakers' bottle brush.

A very old trick for brushless bottle cleaning is to add a handful of split dried peas to the detergent solution in the bottle. Shake in a circular motion, and, nine chances out of ten, all dirt and deposits on the inside of the bottle will be worn away.

Sterilizing washed wine bottles is a must if wine is to keep. I sterilize all of my washed bottles in a very easy way. After a thorough washing in a hot detergent solution, and a thorough rinsing, I put the bottles into a large portable roaster at 250° F. for 30 minutes. The same thing can be done in an oven, if the temperature can be regulated at that degree.

Instead of sterilizing in a roaster, or in the oven, seven bottles at a time can be put in the canner kettle to sterilize; place in the rack, neck down, with about an inch of water at the bottom. Steam sterilize them in this manner for 30 minutes.

When removing the bottles from any sterilizing method, be

sure there is no cold draft blowing, or the result will be bottle and soul shattering.

There is just one rule for putting wine into the bottles: The bottles should always be filled to overflowing. In other words, even when setting the cork in lightly for the period of bottle fermentation, it should rest directly upon the wine in the neck of the bottle. If any overflowing occurs during fermentation in the bottle, the wine will work its way out around the loosely placed cork. If, after fermentation, the level of the wine has gone down, the bottles should again be filled so that the wine is against the cork.

Another thing I do for the preservation of my wine is the paraffin trick. Until you have tried to serve a bottle of wine with bits of wax floating all over the surface, you haven't been mortified. Guests speculate at length about what it could possibly be—it makes you wish you had served root beer. Well, I surmounted the floating-wax problem by taking a lesson from Cheddar cheese. I observed that a piece of cheesecloth had been wrapped around the cheese, before it was dipped in wax, making the peeling off of the outer rind an easy task.

I do the same thing to my wine bottles now, only on a much fancier scale. If I'm bottling grape wine, I use red muslin of the cheapest grade. This I cut in three inch squares with pinking shears. Then I carefully put the center of the cork in the middle of the three-inch square and draw the whole thing down around the neck of the bottle with a matching red rubber band. Then I gently dip the cloth-covered cork and bottle neck in hot paraffin. I do not quite cover all the cloth, but leave the corners sticking out of the paraffin as a color clue to what kind of wine is in the bottle. If the wax is very hot and only a thin coating flows over, I dip twice to form a durable air-tight seal. This method works out beautifully—it not only color codes the wine on the shelves, but the bottles are attractive to the eye.

When opening times comes, it is a real pleasure! All I have to do is slip a paring knife under the waxed cloth and begin prying it off. The whole wax cap comes off in one piece, leaving the cork completely clean and ready to have the corkscrew attack its innards.

I found I could really go all out on this wax-dipping method. One summer I was making Spiced Orange-and-Lemon Christmas Wine (see page 147.) While the wax was still hot and moist, I dipped each bottle head in silver glitter. I had put the wine in dark green bottles with a red-cloth cap for Christmas, and the addition of the glitter made the array look more like the holidays than Santa Claus.

This hot wax-sealing method is really foolproof. It will keep outer contamination away from the corks. However, there is only one precaution: Be absolutely sure the wine is all through fermenting before sealing the bottles with cloth and wax. Explosions are a bothersome climax to a hard day of winemaking.

Labeling wine is perhaps as important as making it. Do not trust to memory, for no matter how good a memory one has, wine in dark bottles can be completely baffling. It is easy to get a young wine instead of an old one off the shelf by mistake. Do not use paper labels which are pasted on, for in time they will dry out and fall off.

Mystik Tape, put out by the Mystik Adhesive Products of Chicago, is a boon to the home winemaker. Here, too, I use the color-code system. I use yellow Mystik Tape to label Dandelion Wine, red tape for Currant, etc. This way you can tell at a glance what is on the shelf, and there is no need to disturb the wine. Mystik Tape is wonderful, too, because you can write on it with a ballpoint pen or plain pencil, putting down the date of bottling and the earliest possible opening date. This tape sticks like fury to glass; there is no chance of a label's falling off.

Being a forgetful soul, I also put a copy of the code colors on the wine-cellar door. If I have just stored away Dandelion Wine with its yellow Mystik Tape label, I take another piece of the same yellow tape and put it on the door with the proper markings.

If the wine is a combination of two kinds of fruit—like Dandelion-Rhubarb Wine—I label each bottle with two strips of tape—one pink to represent the rhubarb, one yellow to represent the dandelions. Mystik Tape comes in a rainbow assortment of colors, and is the only permanent material I have ever found convenient for home winemaking labels.

This about sums up all of the really important tricks I have learned via the experimental route. As you make your own wine, you'll find successful shortcuts and methods. And when you do, I would appreciate hearing about them.

Before starting any recipe, read it carefully and thoroughly all the way through. Then check to be sure that all the necessary ingredients are on hand. (If you've ever followed a recipe from any kind of a cookbook, you probably already know this rule. But it's important enough to be worth emphasizing.)

When reading the recipes, you may wonder why no specific yield is given. This is because there are so many variable factors involved. Humidity or the lack of it in a certain geographic area, the water content of the fruit, and the rate of evaporation, all may alter the amount of wine produced. The recipes are planned to yield *approximately* one gallon, but don't worry if your own result is considerably different.

Incidentally, if you want more wine of a certain kind than one gallon, you may double or triple the amounts given. But don't try to make less than a gallon; if you cut down the ingredients as shown in the recipe, the whole balance will be thrown off.

One last caution: Remember to be scrupulously clean about everything you do, if you expect to have winemaking success at every turn.

By the way, has your winemakers' permit come back in the mail already? Then you are really ready to begin.

CHAPTER IV

Wine from Flower Petals

Dandelions, the scourge of lawns, are a wonderful wine-maker. People are always asking why they are not able to buy dandelion wine on the commercial market. The answer is simple. Of all the wines, this probably involves more painstaking work than any other. Due to the amount of labor involved, commercial wineries couldn't possibly market a dandelion wine that could be sold profitably even at the price of champagne.

I have tasted homemade dandelion wines that almost made me swear gasoline had been siphoned into the bottle by accident. I have tasted others that were sheer ecstasy. There is one secret in making dandelion wine which makes all the difference—the removal of the green material which holds the hundreds of yellow petals in place.

You've observed dandelions after they have gone to seed; there is always a cushionlike button at the end of the stem. This cushion has hundreds of pores into which each little blossom is fastened. When the flower is in its full bloom, this cushion contains the same white sticky fluid as the stem. This fluid makes wine bitter. Holding the flower in the left hand on a cutting board, you can remove this bitter cushion with one cut of a sharp paring knife.

Pick dandelions on a really fine spring day. The sun should be shining and the blooms wide open; they should be picked after all signs of dew have vanished. When this kind of day occurs, and the lawns and fields are dotted with golden yellow, begin.

Pick the open blossoms and pile them lightly into baskets. Do not put too many blossoms in one basket, as the weight of the blossoms will crush them and cause wilting. This will make the green more difficult to remove. The very same day that the blossoms are picked, they should be shorn of their green and the wine should be started. Any delay between picking and cleaning will only result in harder work and a mild form of failure.

If the blossoms are dusty, wash them in cold running water before removing the green material. If it's one of those years when the ant population is high, it is always wise to give the blossoms a quick washing. The best method is to use a laundry tub full of cold water, putting in several quarts of blossoms at a time and working them up and down gently for a few seconds. Then remove by the handful to a board to drain. This will leave any stowaway ants swimming around in circles.

The abundance of dandelions seems infinite when you're trying to get them out of the lawn, but the moment you start gathering them for wine they get as scarce as wild strawberries. If there is a park nearby with pretty lawns, ask the caretaker when he intends to mow the grass and get there the day before; he will probably love you for scalping those baskets of blooms from his lawn.

A golf course is another ideal place for a dandelion harvest. And I know one gent who reaps a dandy dandelion harvest in a local cemetery, but this is not for me. For some reason the dandelions that grow in wild abandon in the farmer's field are bigger than the golf course, park or cemetery variety—probably due to tilled or fertilized soil. Naturally, the bigger the flower heads, the less bending and cleaning involved in the task.

The following recipes are for a little over a gallon of dandelion wine. However, if the blooms are in great supply, please make more than a gallon. After the first sip the hours of stooping down and picking in the hot sun will hold no regrets!

PLAIN DANDELION WINE

1st week:
4 quarts of dandelion flowers, cleaned of all their green
4 quarts of boiling water
2nd week:
4 oranges cut in 1/4" slices
4 lemons cut in 1/4" slices
1 cup of white raisins, finely chopped
6 cups of cane sugar
1 package of dry granulated yeast
Put dandelion blossoms in canner kettle and pour the

boiling water over them. Let stand in a warm place for one week. Stir twice a day if possible.

At the end of the week, strain the blossoms through a jelly bag, squeezing the pulp very dry to extract all of the liquid and flavor.

Return liquid to the canner kettle and add the sliced oranges and lemons, and the raisins. Stir in the sugar; be sure to stir long enough to dissolve every grain. Sprinkle the dry granulated yeast over the surface. Set in a warm place to ferment for two weeks. Stir every day, inverting the fruit which rises to the surface.

At the end of this two-week period, strain through several thicknesses of cheesecloth, and return to canner kettle to settle for two days more.

When the wine has settled, siphon off carefully into clean sterilized bottles. Put corks in lightly until all fermentation is over. Fermentation has stopped when small bubbles no longer cling to the sides of the bottles. Then tighten the corks securely and dip in hot paraffin. Let wine age at least six months; it is best at the end of a year. In aging dandelion wine, your resistance to the temptation of sampling will govern the quality of the wine.

In the spring when dandelions start to bloom again, the wine will go through a slight fermentation in the bottle; it will become a little turbid and cloudy. Don't be alarmed, for it will settle back after the dandelions are through blooming.

DANDELION-PINEAPPLE WINE

Here is a union of two flavors which make a delightfully different dessert wine. It is sweet but, as a rule, not too sweet even for those who prefer dry wines.

1st week:

4 quarts of dandelion blossoms, cleaned of all green

4 quarts of boiling water

2nd week:

1 orange cut in ¼" slices

1 lemon cut in ¼" slices

1 large very ripe pineapple, or 2 #2 cans crushed pineapple

8 cups of cane sugar

1 slice of white toast

1 ounce of wet yeast

Clean the dandelions as directed in the recipe for Plain Dandelion Wine; put blossoms into canner kettle with the boiling water, and ferment for one week. At the end of this week, strain through jelly bag, squeezing well to extract all of the flavor and liquid.

Remove stem from pineapple, but do not peel or remove the core. Slice into pieces which will lend themselves to chopping, and chop as fine as coleslaw. Put chopped pineapple and dandelion liquid into canner kettle with sliced oranges and lemons. Stir in the sugar, making sure all of it dissolves. Moisten the yeast with a few drops of water, and spread on the surface of the toast. Float the toast, yeast side down, on the surface of the liquid. Set aside in a warm place to ferment for two weeks. Stir daily, pushing down any fruit which rises to the top.

At the end of this two-week fermentation period, strain through several thicknesses of cheesecloth and return to the canner kettle to settle for two days more. At the end of this settling period, siphon off into clean dry bottles. Cork lightly, watching closely for the fermentation to cease. When it is over, cork tightly and seal with paraffin. Keep for at least six months but, like Plain Dandelion Wine, this is much better if aged for a year.

Dandelion-Pineapple Wine makes an excellent drink if served with seltzer water and ice. Another favorite of ours is Dandelion-Pineapple Wine over the rocks; we use large Old-Fashioned glasses. We put 4 ice cubes into these glasses and fill the rest up with wine. This is a marvelous companion for those hot summer afternoons when the most strenuous thing you care to do is just sit.

DANDELION-RHUBARB-PINEAPPLE WINE

1st week:
3 quarts of dandelion blossoms, cleaned of all their green
4 quarts of boiling water
2nd week:
4 quarts of cut-up rhubarb, cut in 1/2" pieces. Use stalks only; see Chapter IX on poisonous quality of rhubarb leaves.
1 large, very ripe pineapple, or 2 #2 cans crushed pineapple

8 cups of cane sugar
1 slice of white toast
1 ounce of wet yeast

Clean dandelions as directed for Plain Dandelion Wine; put into canner kettle and pour boiling water over them. Let stand for one week. At the end of this week, strain through a jelly bag, squeezing dry to extract all of the liquid and flavor. Return liquid to canner kettle, reserving 2 cups to dissolve the sugar.

Remove the top stem of the pineapple, and cut into slices convenient for chopping. Do not peel. Chop fine as for coleslaw and add to the dandelion liquid with a cut-up rhubarb. Put the sugar and the 2 cups of dandelion liquid into a saucepan and melt over a low flame. Be sure to stir to prevent scorching. While still hot, add to the dandelion-fruit mixture, stirring well so all is mixed. Moisten the yeast with a little water and spread on one side of the toast. Float toast yeast side down on the surface of the liquid. Put in warm place to ferment for two weeks. Stir daily.

At the end of two-week period, strain through jelly bag, squeezing very dry, and return to canner kettle to settle for two days more. Then siphon off into clean, sterilized bottles and cork lightly until fermentation stops. When fermentation is definitely over, cork tightly and seal with paraffin. Keep for at least six months.

DANDELION-ELDERBERRY FLOWER WINE

1st three days:
2 quarts of dandelion blossoms, cleaned of all their green
2 quarts of elderberry flowers; *omit all large fleshy stems*
8 cups of cane sugar
4 quarts of water
final step:
1 slice of white toast
1 ounce of wet yeast

Clean dandelions as directed for Plain Dandelion Wine and put into canner kettle. Add elderberry flowers; small stems only, as large ones will give the wine a bitter taste. Bring 3 quarts of the water to a boil and pour over the combined flower blossoms. Set in a warm place overnight. The following day, dissolve the sugar in the 1 remaining quart of water over a low flame. While still warm, add to flower solution.

38

Stir well, pushing all blossoms to the bottom. Let ferment together for three more days.

At the end of the third day, strain through jelly bag, squeezing well to extract all the liquid and flavor. Return to canner kettle. Moisten yeast with a little water and spread on one side of the toast. Float the toast, yeast side down, on the surface of liquid. Let stand in a warm place for two weeks without disturbing.

At the end of the two-week period, strain through several thicknesses of cheesecloth and return to the canner kettle to settle for two days more. Siphon off into clean sterilized bottles and cork lightly. When no more little bubbles appear on sides of bottles, fermentation has ceased. Then cork tightly and seal with paraffin. Keep for six months; however, a year makes this wine still more wonderful.

ELDERBERRY BLOSSOM WINE

Elderberry blossoms, like dandelions, should be picked after all dew has been dried by the sun. Be sure to pick only the webby portion of the blossoms. Leave all large fleshy stalks on the bush, for these will make the wine bitter. When picking elderberry blossoms, take along good sharp scissors—they will save you time. Too, by cutting with scissors, the main budding sections of the bush are preserved, so that you can go back to the same bush next year.

4 quarts of elderberry blossoms (loosely packed)
4 quarts of boiling water
6 cups of cane sugar
3 oranges cut in 1/4" slices
3 lemons cut in 1/4" slices
1 package of dry granulated yeast

Put elderberry blossoms into bottom of the canner kettle and pour boiling water over them. While this is still warm, stir in sugar, stirring well so that every grain is dissolved. Add sliced lemons and oranges, stirring again, so that they are held down in the elderberry flowers and not floating on top. Sprinkle the dry granulated yeast over the surface. Set in a warm place to ferment for four weeks. Stir twice a week during this period so that the blossoms which rise to the top are pushed back into the liquid.

At the end of this four-week period, strain through the jelly bag, squeezing gently, so that the bitterness of the flower stem is not squeezed into the wine. Return to canner kettle to settle for three days more. In siphoning this wine, keep the hose off the bottom of the kettle, or cloudy material will be drawn up. Measure the depth of the kettle from the outside, then tape the hose in place in the kettle (with adhesive or Mystik Tape) so that it is just off the bottom. Siphon all of the clear wine into clean sterilized bottles and cork lightly. When fermentation has ceased, cork tightly and seal with paraffin. The wine left with the settlings in the bottom of the kettle can be poured off into a fruit jar for further settling; then the clear wine from this can be siphoned off into another bottle. Elderberry Blossom Wine should be kept for at least six months. If you can resist its lure for a whole year, so much the better.

TAWNY ELDERBERRY FLOWER WINE

Here is a good recipe to follow if you have only a small amount of elderberry blossoms.

4 cups of elderberry blossoms
4 quarts of water
6 cups of cane sugar
2 lemons cut into 1/4" slices
3 cups of muscat raisins, finely chopped
1 package of dry granulated yeast

In this case, the elderberry flowers have to be snipped off with as little stem as possible. Put them into the bottom of the canner kettle, add the water and bring to a slow rolling boil for 30 minutes. Remove from fire and stir in the sugar, being sure that it is all dissolved. Add sliced lemons and chopped raisins. When the liquid is lukewarm, sprinkle the dry granulated yeast over the surface. Set in a warm place to ferment for two weeks. Stir every day, pushing to the bottom any fruit or blossoms which may rise.

At the end of this two-week period, strain through jelly bag, squeezing well, so that all the liquid and flavor are out of the mash. Return to the canner kettle to settle for two more days.

After this settling period, siphon off into clean sterilized bottles and cork lightly for one week. Then fasten the corks tightly and seal with paraffin. This is a "quickie" wine that is ready for use in 90 days; naturally, the longer you keep it the better it is.

ELDERBERRY BLOSSOM-RHUBARB WINE

4 quarts of elderberry blossoms (no heavy stems, please!)
4 quarts of rhubarb, cut into ½" pieces (see Chapter IX)
1 orange cut into ¼" slices
1 lemon cut into ¼" slices
4 quarts of room-temperature water
8 cups of cane sugar (to be added after two weeks)

Put elderberry blossoms, rhubarb, oranges and lemons into canner kettle. Then add the room-temperature water. Set in a warm place to ferment for two weeks. Here is the backbreaker: Stir twice a day, inverting the fruit and flowers. That is, completely turn over the mash, reversing the top to the bottom each time you stir.

At the end of this two-week period drain through jelly bag, squeezing well so that all liquid is extracted. Put the sugar into a saucepan with two cups of the strained liquid. Heat this over a low flame, stirring frequently to prevent scorching. Bring to a boil, then add to the elderberry blossom-rhubarb liquid. Set aside in a warm place to ferment for two weeks longer without disturbing.

At the end of this second two-week period (that's four weeks in all) strain through several thicknesses of cheesecloth and return to the canner kettle to settle for two more days. Then siphon off into clean sterilized bottles and cork lightly until fermentation has ceased. When you are sure it is over, cork tightly and seal with paraffin. This wine *must* be kept ten months before opening, or you will be disappointed. The flavor reward is worth every minute of the waiting period.

Cowslip Flowers

The cowslip is to spring and early summer what colored leaves are to autumn. Anyone who has ever hiked through country fields on a chilly spring day has come across fields resplendent with cowslip blossoms. From the standpoint of the winemaker, they choose most inconvenient places to grow. Usually they are bowing and beckoning from the middle of a muddy, oozy lowland. But the excellence of the wine repays you for the time spent in scraping thick globs of mud off your shoes. Here are two fine wines from these beautiful little flowers (which should be gathered with a minimum of green on them).

SIMPLE COWSLIP WINE

1st two weeks:
4 quarts of cowslip flowers
4 quarts of cold water
final step:
8 cups of cane sugar
4 crushed eggshells (these are used in the second stage of the wine, so you can save them from your cooking)

When picking cowslips, do not pack too many in the same container; their weight will crush them. They should be packed very lightly, since they are fragile flowers. Please notice that it takes one quart of water and two cups of sugar to every quart of blossoms. Should you pick more or less than the recipe, you can adjust the measurements according to this ratio.

Put the cowslip blossoms into canner kettle and pour the cold water over them. Let flowers ferment in water for two weeks. Stir daily, but very gently, or you will make your wine turbid. While stirring, examine the liquid, and if any of the blossoms look spoiled, remove them from the mash with a slotted spoon.

At the end of this two weeks' fermentation of flowers and water, strain them through the jelly bag, squeezing gently enough to remove the liquid only. Add two cups of this liquid to the sugar in a saucepan. Put over a low flame and stir until dissolved. Then remove from the fire. Set aside to cool to lukewarm, then add to the liquid in canner kettle. Put in a warm place to ferment for an additional ten days. At the end of this period, sprinkle crushed eggshells over the surface and let settle and clear for four more days.

After this second fermentation-clearing period (this totals four weeks in all) siphon into clean sterilized bottles. Do not put the siphoning hose at the bottom of the kettle, but tape in place. The eggshells and cloudy wine at the bottom should be thrown away. This wine should be aged for at least six months. However, Cowslip Wine that has been aged for eighteen months is incomparable.

FORTIFIED COWSLIP WINE

4 quarts of clowslip flowers (cut away all the green material)
4 quarts of boiling water
8 cups of cane sugar
2 oranges cut into 1/4" slices
2 lemons cut into 1/4" slices
1 package of dry granulated yeast
1 cup of domestic grape brandy (added later)

Put the flower heads, sugar, sliced oranges and lemons into canner kettle. Pour over all 4 quarts of boiling water. Stir in a gentle circular motion to dissolve all the sugar. Try not to crush the blossoms while stirring. Set aside to cool to lukewarm. When lukewarm (test on your wrist), sprinkle the dry yeast over the surface. Allow to ferment in a warm place for four days.

After this period, strain through jelly bag, squeezing gently to extract only the liquid. Then return to canner kettle and set in a warm place for two weeks more of fermentation.

When this second fermentation period is up, strain through several thicknesses of cheesecloth. Return to the canner kettle and add one cup of brandy. Let stand for two more days to settle. Then siphon off into clean sterilized bottles. Cork lightly at first. When fermentation has ceased, fasten the corks tightly, and dip in paraffin. This wine will be ready in four months, but the longer you keep it, the better it is.

If You're Ever in Clover—

When my mother told me about the birds and the bees she made no mention about why bees are always found in a field of clover. If they are taking the nectar home for honey and homemade wines, I can understand why they are so busy. It's easy to understand, too, why they lose their tempers when a mere human strides through their purple, pink and white paradise.

The day you pick cloverheads for wine has to be a beauty— like the day you chose for dandelion picking. The sun must be shining, and the dew must be gone. Pick the purple and white heads in the same manner as the dandelions—plucking them off with two fingers just below the blossoms. Try not to get too many leaves, etc. with the blooms. Put in a large ventilated wicker basket or a similar receptacle, so air can circulate. When you get the blooms home, spread them out in the sun on a piece of old sheeting till they wilt. If this is not possible and they must be left overnight, turn them over once or twice before going to bed. This will permit those at the bottom to dry out as evenly as those at the top. Pick over the blossoms, breaking off any surplus green, and you are ready to begin your wine.

CLOVER WINE

8 quarts of wilted and dried clover blossoms
4 quarts of boiling water
8 cups of cane sugar
3 lemons cut into ¼" slices
3 oranges cut into ¼" slices
¼ lb. of candied ginger, finely chopped
1 package of dry granulated yeast

Put the clover blossoms into the canner kettle; then pour the boiling water over them. Put the kettle over a low flame and simmer slowly for two hours. Set aside to cool to luke-warm, then strain through jelly bag, squeezing well so that all the liquid is extracted. Return liquid to canner kettle, then stir in the sugar, making sure all is dissolved. Add the sliced lemons and oranges and the candied ginger. Sprinkle the dry yeast over the surface. Put in a warm place to ferment for two weeks. After the second day of fermentation, stir well. Thereafter it is necessary to stir twice a week only.

After this two-week fermentation period, strain through several thicknesses of cheesecloth. Then return to the canner kettle to settle for two days more. Siphon off into clean sterilized bottles and cork lightly. This wine goes through quite a gay period in the bottle, so be very careful not to cork it too early. When there are no more signs of bubbles on the sides of the bottle, fasten the corks tightly and seal with paraffin. Keep for at least three months.

Coltsfoot Flowers

The coltsfoot flower is a yellow sunflower-shaped bloom belonging to the aster family. Its formal name is *Tussilago farfara*. It grows in wild abandon in many regions of the

44

United States. But all yellow flowers shaped like sunflowers do not make good wine. If not sure they are coltsfoot flowers, ask your State Agricultural Department to identify them before you pick them. This service costs nothing.

COLTSFOOT WINE

8 cups (tightly packed) of coltsfoot flowers
2 oranges
2 lemons
8 cups of cane sugar
1 cup of white raisins, finely chopped
4 quarts of water
1 package of dry granulated yeast

Peel oranges and lemons with a potato peeler, just as you would potatoes. Set aside fruit. Put peelings and coltsfoot flowers into canner kettle. Add finely chopped raisins. Dissolve sugar in 2 quarts of water over a low flame; bring to a rapid boil and, while still boiling hot, pour over blossoms and fruit. Set aside in a warm place overnight.

The following day, squeeze oranges and lemons and add the strained juice to the contents of the canner kettle. Bring the remaining 2 quarts of water to a rapid boil and add to the mash. Sprinkle the dry granulated yeast over the surface. Put in a warm place to ferment for one week.

Then strain through a jelly bag, squeezing quite dry. Return the liquid to the canner kettle to settle for two days longer.

Then siphon off into clean sterilized bottles. Be careful, in siphoning, to keep the hose off the bottom and out of the settled material. Cork lightly until fermentation has ceased. When you are sure it is over, cork bottle tightly and seal with paraffin. Keep this wine for at least six months. Keeping it a year will give you deeper flavor and color.

Clary Blossoms

The common clary blossom is a member of the sage family. Botanically it is classified as *Salvia sclarea*. The clary plant was brought to the United States and cultivated in gardens, but escaped these confines and now grows wild in the older settled parts of the United States. However, gardens in very old sections of our country still have an abundance of clary plants. At one time they were used as a heart remedy, and for centuries they have been used as a flavoring agent. If you want to do your picking from a wild patch, be sure that you know they are definitely clary blossoms. If there is any doubt in your mind, send a sample to your State Agricultural Department. (I shall not attempt to give a description of clary blossoms here, for they range in color from deep purple to gray white; in some regions they grow quite high, and in others they hug the ground, moss fashion.)

CLARY BLOSSOM WINE

4 cups of tightly packed clary blossoms (tops only)
2 cups of raisins, finely chopped
6 cups of cane sugar
4 quarts of water
1 package of dry granulated yeast

Pick clary blossoms on a clear, dry day. Then spread them on old sheeting in the sun for several hours to wilt and dry. Put sugar and water into canner kettle over a low flame. When the sugar is completely dissolved, bring to a rolling boil. Remove from fire and immediately sprinkle in the clary blossoms. Stir well so that all the blossoms are thoroughly wet. Set aside to cool to lukewarm.

When you are sure the blossoms and water are lukewarm, stir in the finely chopped raisins. Sprinkle the dry yeast over the surface and set in a warm place to ferment for one week. Do *not* stir during this week of fermentation.

At the end of this week, strain through jelly bag, and return to canner kettle to ferment for an additional two-week period.

At the end of this fermentation (this is three weeks in all, so far) strain through several thicknesses of cheesecloth. No additional settling period is needed for this wine; it can be siphoned into clean sterilized bottles immediately after this last straining. Cork lightly until fermentation has ceased; then cork tightly and seal with paraffin. Keep for at least six months.

Burnet Flowers

Burnet flowers are another import into the United States. They are a familiar sight in old gardens in the South and

46

in the Middle Atlantic states. Burnets belong to the rose family and are classified under the name *Sanguisorba*. Some plants have escaped from the gardens and have grown wild, but for the most part the cultivated burnet is best for wine. When making Burnet Wine, use only the flower heads. Again, if using wild burnets, be sure you definitely know them. If there is even a remote doubt, have your State Agricultural Department identify them.

HEAVY BURNET WINE

    4 quarts of burnet flowers
    4 quarts of water
    3 oranges
    3 lemons
    8 cups of cane sugar
    1 cup of white raisins
    1 package of dry granulated yeast

Peel oranges and lemons as thin as possible with a potato peeler; set aside for two days. Put the peelings and burnet flowers into canner kettle. Bring 3 quarts of the water to a rapid rolling boil, and then pour over the blossoms and peelings. Leave in a warm place for two days. Stir once or twice, making sure that the flowers are submerged and turned over.

When the two days have passed, dissolve the sugar in the remaining quart of water and bring to a boil for five minutes. Cool to lukewarm. While cooling, strain the burnet flowers and fruit peelings through jelly bag, squeezing quite dry. Return the liquid to canner kettle. Squeeze juice from the peeled oranges and lemons and add the juice to the burnet liquid.

When the sugar has cooled to lukewarm, stir in. Add finely chopped white raisins. Sprinkle the yeast over the surface and set in a warm place to ferment for two more weeks.

At the end of this period, strain through several thicknesses of cheesecloth and return to canner kettle to settle for one more week. Then siphon off into clean sterilized bottles and cork lightly. When signs of fermentation have disappeared, cork tightly and seal with paraffin. Keep for at least six months.

Almost any flower that has a pleasant fragrance can be turned into fine wine. Naturally, one should not go out and pick the highly poisonous purple nightshade because it is so pretty. If there is any cultivated flower that seems a likely winemaking subject, find out first if it is nonpoisonous by sending samples to your State Agricultural Department. By no means venture to make wine of any flower not properly identified and investigated.

Before wasting good time and materials, ask these questions about the blossoms being considered for wine: Is the fragrance fine and steady? Is there any hint of extreme bitterness? Are they nonpoisonous? If you don't care for experimentation, the following recipes have all been tried and found to be excellent.

CARNATION WINE
(Pinks are in the carnation family too)

1st week:
4 quarts of carnations, shorn of their green material
3 quarts of water
2nd week:
6 cups of cane sugar
1 orange cut in 1/4" slices
1 lemon cut in 1/4" slices
2 cups of muscat raisins, finely chopped
1 ounce of wet yeast
1 slice of white toast

Put flowers into canner kettle. Bring water to a rapid boil and pour over flowers. Put in a warm place for one week. Stir every day, inverting flowers so that those on top are pushed to the bottom. At the end of this week, strain through jelly bag. Reserve 2 cups of liquid for dissolving the sugar. Add oranges, lemons and raisins. Put the sugar into a saucepan with the 2 cups of liquid. Place over a low flame and stir until sugar is all dissolved. Then bring to a boil. While still hot, add to flower and fruit mixture. Moisten the yeast with a few drops of water and spread on the toast. Float the toast, yeast side down, on the surface of the liquid. Set in a warm place to ferment for four additional weeks without disturbing.

At the end of this period, strain through several thicknesses of cheesecloth. Return to canner kettle to settle for two days more. Then siphon off into clean sterilized bottles and cork lightly. When fermentation is over, cork tightly and seal with paraffin. Keep for at least three months; however, it improves greatly with age.

Daisies

Besides never telling very much, and being present in every junior prom corsage, daisies always seemed rather uninteresting to me, until I tasted my first glass of daisy wine. If you find a field of daisies bowing to the sun—start picking! This chore is less backbreaking than gathering dandelions, because daisies grow taller. Here again, each bloom must have the bottom green removed or bitter wine will result.

DAISY WINE

1st stage:
8 quarts of field or cultivated daisies
4 quarts of boiling water
2nd stage:
3 lemons cut into ¼" slices
8 cups of brown sugar
2 cups of muscat raisins, finely chopped
1 package of dry granulated yeast
8 to 10 peppercorns (optional)

Try to avoid washing the daisies; however, if they are dusty, rinse them in cold running water. Let drain on several thicknesses of toweling. Then put them into canner kettle and pour the boiling water over them. Let stand for one whole day and night. Then strain through jelly bag, squeezing very dry to extract all the liquid. Return the liquid to canner kettle; add sliced lemons. Take 3 cups of daisy liquid and dissolve the sugar in it over a low flame, then bring to a boil. While still hot, add to the rest of the daisy liquid. Add chopped raisins; sprinkle the dry granulated yeast over the surface. Set in a warm place to ferment for two weeks without disturbing.

At the end of this period, strain again through jelly bag, squeezing very dry to extract all the liquid. Return to canner kettle to settle for two days more, then siphon into clean sterilized bottles. Avoid putting the siphoning hose to the very bottom of the kettle, for this will rouse up the settled material and make your wine cloudy. Cork the bottles lightly until you are sure fermentation has ceased. Then cork tightly and seal with paraffin. Keep for at least four months.

This is an excellent amber wine with fine flavor. If made in June, it is ready in October when there is a nip in the air and a glass of warming wine is welcome. If you want to make this wine warmer, add 8 or 10 peppercorns at the same time as the raisins. It is good either way.

Marigolds

Marigolds are a favorite in my garden because they take so little care. They are marvelous, too, in that they flourish from Maine to California. Their cheerful golden-rust heads dress up a garden. Aside from being a wonderful cut flower for the house, the marigold is a wonderful source for rich, deeply flavored wine. Imagine, all this from a ten-cent package of seeds! Marigold blossoms should be shorn of their bottom green just as dandelions and daisies are. Here are three Marigold Wine recipes which will mystify your guests.

PLAIN MARIGOLD WINE

1st week:
1 quart (tightly packed) of marigold flower tops
4 quarts of tepid water
2nd week:
6 cups of cane sugar
2 cups of cracked whole wheat, toasted a golden brown
1 cup of muscat raisins
1 package of dry granulated yeast

Put flowers into canner kettle and add the water. Put in a warm place for one week. Stir every day and invert the flowers which rise to the top. During this time, if any blooms have spoiled, remove immediately with a slotted spoon.

At the end of one week, toast the wheat by spreading it in a shallow pan and placing in a 375° F. oven for 30 minutes, or until golden brown. Meanwhile, strain the marigold liquid through jelly bag, squeezing well to extract all the liquid. Return liquid to canner kettle, reserving 3 cups in which to dissolve the sugar. Put sugar in a saucepan with the 3 cups of liquid, and dissolve over a low flame. Bring to a boil and add to the marigold liquid along with the raisins and hot cracked wheat. Test the liquid on your wrist to be sure that it is not too hot for the yeast. (It should be just lukewarm.) Then sprinkle the yeast over the surface. Set in a warm place to ferment for two weeks. Stir twice a week.

At the end of this period, strain through several thicknesses of cheesecloth. Return to canner kettle to settle for two days more. Then siphon off into clean sterilized bottles, and cork lightly. When fermentation has ceased, cork tightly and seal with paraffin. If this wine is made in August when the marigolds are at their best, mark each bottle with "Do Not Open Until Christmas—" that's when it will be at its very best. This is a wonderful Christmas wine; its pungent flavor is a welcome change from all the sweets which appear in every household during the holidays.

SWEET MARIGOLD WINE

1st week:
2 quarts of marigold flowers, tightly packed
8 quarts of cold water
2nd week:
4 cups of cane sugar
2 lbs. of honey
2 oranges cut into 1/4" slices
2 lemons cut into 1/4" slices
2 cups of white raisins, finely chopped
1 ounce of wet yeast
1 slice of white toast

Put flowers into canner kettle, after stripping them of their green material; add cold water and let stand for one week. During this time, look for signs of any flower spoilage; remove any spoiled ones from mash with a slotted spoon. Strain through jelly bag, squeezing well to remove liquid. Add oranges, lemons, raisins. Dissolve the sugar in 2 cups of marigold liquid. Put over a low flame and, when hot, add the honey. Bring to a boil for 5 minutes. Remove scum from the top. While still hot, add to liquid in canner kettle. Spread the slightly moistened yeast on one side of toast, and float, yeast side down, on the surface of the liquid. Put in a warm place to ferment for three weeks. Stir twice a week.

At the end of this period, strain again through jelly bag, squeezing well to extract all liquid. Siphon into clean sterilized bottles immediately and cork lightly. When fermentation has ceased, cork tightly and seal with paraffin. Keep this wine for at least six months.

MARIGOLD-AND-RHUBARB WINE

Here is a good use for that tough end-of-the-garden rhubarb which is usually too mature for eating.

1st two weeks:

1 quart of marigold blossoms

3 quarts of cut-up rhubarb, cut in ½" pieces (use stalks only!—see Chapter IX regarding the poisonous quality of the leaves)

4 quarts of cold water

final stage:

6 cups of cane sugar

1 lb. of honey

After removing the green from marigolds, combine them with cut-up rhubarb in the canner kettle. Cover with the cold water; put in a warm place to ferment for two weeks. Stir every day, removing any spoiled blossoms with a slotted spoon. At the end of this two-week period, strain through jelly bag. Reserve 2 cups of the liquid to dissolve the sugar. Place sugar in a saucepan with the 2 cups of liquid over a low flame and stir until all the sugar is dissolved. When just below the boiling point, add honey and bring to a boil for 5 minutes. Skim off any scum which may come to the surface. While still hot, add to the flower-rhubarb mixture. Set in a warm place to ferment for two weeks.

At the end of this period, strain through several thicknesses of cheesecloth, then return to the canner kettle to settle for two days more. Then siphon off into clean sterilized bottles, corking lightly until fermentation has ceased. When you are sure it is over, cork tightly and seal with paraffin. Keep for six months; however, a year makes this a wonderful wine.

There are many more recipes for flower wines; you will even find additional ones in other portions of this book. See the chapter on citrus fruits for Orange, Lemon, and Lime Blossom Wine; also see the chapter called "Meads, or Wines Made with Honey." If you have any flower wine recipes which are good, I hope you will pass them along to me.

CHAPTER V

Wine from Wild Berries

Almost every summer there is a harrowing newspaper account of somebody's being lost in the woods for days on end. After the rescue, and while in the comforting confines of the local hospital, getting warm food and rest, the victim is usually asked by the press to talk about his experience. The first question invariably is, "What did you eat?" The reply is almost always, "Oh, I lived on berries and drank water from streams."

There are many delicious berries thriving in our woods. Usually they bloom, produce their fruit, and go to seed—all for want of somebody to pick them. In this chapter, I am going to deal with only the most familiar of berries and how to make wine out of them.

The Choke Cherry

The choke cherry is a friend of almost all children. Most of us can recall returning from a hike with our mouths puckered and purple and our clothing hopelessly stained because we'd found a bush of choke cherries. In the spring this bush blooms with fragrant finger-shaped clusters of cream-colored blossoms that have a wonderful odor.

When the choke cherries are as dark as Bing cherries, they are ready to make into wine. You can pick them in two ways: Either pick the fingerlike clusters, stems and all, and strip them off later at home, or hold a small container under the cluster and strip it clean right on the bush. I prefer the first method if there is to be a long wait between picking and winemaking. The stems act as packing material and prevent the fruit from getting crushed.

Choke cherries have a penchant for growing along roadways. Dust is usually very abundant during their ripe season. If the fruit is dusty and gritty, it may be rinsed quickly under cold running water. Then the fruit should be drained carefully on several layers of toweling.

CHOKE CHERRY WINE

1st two weeks:
4 quarts of ripe choke cherries
4 quarts of water
2nd two weeks:
8 cups of cane sugar
2 cups of raisins, finely chopped
1 package of dry granulated yeast

Put the picked-over choke cherries into the canner kettle and crush lightly with a potato masher. Bring 4 quarts of water to a rapid boil and immediately pour over the crushed fruit. Set in a warm place to ferment for two weeks. Stir and crush the fruit against the sides of the canner kettle once a day.

At the end of this two-week period, strain through the jelly bag, squeezing well so that all the juice and flavor is extracted. Reserve 2 cups of the liquid to dissolve the sugar, and return the rest to the canner kettle. Add the finely chopped raisins. Dissolve the sugar in a saucepan with the 2 cups of liquid over a low flame. Bring to a rapid boil for 5 minutes. Add this sugar mixture to the choke cherry liquid while still boiling hot. Stir all very well, to mix. Sprinkle the dry granulated yeast over the surface. Set in a warm place to ferment for two weeks longer. No more stirring is necessary.

At the end of this second fermentation period, strain through several thicknesses of cheesecloth and return to the canner kettle to settle for two days more. Then siphon into clean sterilized bottles and cork lightly. When fermentation has ceased, cork tightly and seal with paraffin. Keep this wine for six months.

Choke Cherry Wine is excellent served over ice as a warm-weather drink. It also lends itself well to fruit salads, and putting a half cup into French dressing will give the dressing a distinctive and delicious touch. A favorite of ours, too, is making jelly molds of Choke Cherry Wine and putting them around a platter of spring lamb or prime beef. But, by the glass, this wine is something special by itself!

DARK CHOKE CHERRY WINE
(Sun-Extraction Method)

4 quarts of choke cherries

54

4 quarts of water
8 cups of dark brown cane sugar

Here, we rely on the sun and on the natural yeast cells already on the choke cherries to perform the miracle of fermentation. You can use 3 two-quart fruit jars or 2 one-gallon jars for this sun-extraction method. Fill each jar about three-quarters full of picked-over choke cherries; then fill up the rest with cold water. Place a small square of plastic over the mouth of each jar, and turn the cap very lightly. Put the jars on the sunny side of the house or garage to ferment without disturbing for two weeks.

At the end of this period, strain the contents of each jar into the canner kettle through the jelly bag. Squeeze the pulp well, to get all the coloring and flavor. Add the dark brown sugar and stir until it is all dissolved. Put in a warm place to ferment for two weeks more.

Then strain through several thicknesses of cheesecloth, and siphon immediately into clean sterilized bottles. Cork lightly at first. Watch the wine carefully, and when you are sure fermentation is over, cork tightly and seal with paraffin. Keep for at least four months. This makes a heavier darker wine than the first choke cherry recipe.

CHOKE-CHERRY-AND-APPLE WINE

4 quarts of choke cherries
4 quarts of crab apples, or any other tart variety of apples
2 cups of muscat raisins, finely chopped
1 cup of plain barley (not pearled)
4 quarts of water
8 cups of dark brown cane sugar

Pick over choke cherries and put into the canner kettle. If any apples have brown spots, this will help fermentation. Chop up apples as fine as coleslaw, and add to the choke cherries. Add the finely chopped raisins and the barley. Then add the 4 quarts of water, and put in a warm place to ferment for four weeks. The mixture should be stirred every day during this period. Be sure to invert the fruit—that is, turn the top to the bottom.

At the end of this period, strain through the jelly bag, squeezing very dry to extract all the juice and flavor. Return the liquid to canner kettle and stir in the dark brown sugar, making sure every grain is dissolved. Set in a warm place to ferment again for two weeks more.

Then strain through several thicknesses of cheesecloth. Return to the canner kettle to settle for one week more. Then siphon off into clean sterilized bottles and cork lightly until fermentation has ceased. When you are sure fermentation is over, cork tightly and seal with paraffin. Keep for at least six months.

CHOKE-CHERRY-AND-QUINCE WINE

1st two weeks:
4 quarts of choke cherries
5 lbs. of quince
4 quarts of water
2nd two weeks:
8 cups of cane sugar
2 cups of muscat raisins

Put picked-over choke cherries into canner kettle. Cut quince in quarters and then chop as fine as coleslaw. Add chopped quince to the choke cherries, along with the water. Put in a warm place to ferment for two weeks. Stir every day during this period.

Then strain through jelly bag, squeezing quite dry to extract all the liquid and flavor. Reserve 2 cups of the liquid and return the rest to the canner kettle. Put the sugar into a saucepan with the 2 cups of liquid and dissolve over a low flame. Add hot liquid with the finely chopped raisins to the contents of the canner kettle. Put in a warm place to ferment for two weeks more. At the end of this time, strain through several thicknesses of cheesecloth, then return to the canner kettle to settle for one additional week.

After the settling period, siphon off into clean sterilized bottles. Cork lightly until fermentation has ceased; then cork tightly and seal with paraffin. This wine should be kept at least eight months. The flavor and bouquet is a real reward for the waiting.

Hawthorn or Thornapple

Hawthorn apples or thornapples grow almost everywhere. There are several thousand varieties in the world. In the United States alone more than one thousand different kinds have been recorded. The fruit ranges in diameter from the size of a small pea to almost an inch. The color is almost as varied as the size, ranging from orange-white through red-black. None of the thousand identified varieties are poisonous —however, if in doubt, send a sample to your State Agricultural Department before making wine from them.

The Europeans utilize the thornapple in more ways than we do. For one thing, they use thorn hedges as field separators, or as natural fences. The sharp spikes discourage wandering cattle, and the bushes grow close to the ground, preventing wind drift of seeds at harvest time.

In the United States, we do not concentrate our thornapple bushes into hedges. The plant is scattered in a wild state from Maine to California. With most of our cities outgrowing their limits and spreading to the outskirts, more and more householders find wild thornapples which missed the onslaught of the bulldozer in their yards. When cultivated and cared for, these bushes are lovely in blossom, and if given fertilizer and the proper spraying, the fruit grows firmer and larger year after year.

The fruit of the thornapple closely resembles the crab apple, both in taste and texture. If you know where there is a thornapple bush, by all means make a date with it for the harvest season. Thornapple Wine is golden in color and wonderful in flavor.

In England there is a variety of thornapple whose double blossom has a wonderful odor. These blossoms make excellent wine. Alas, the single blossoms of the American varieties of thornapple do not, it was my sad experience to learn.

THORNAPPLE WINE

1st four weeks:
4 quarts of thornapples
4 quarts of water
1 cup of muscat raisins
½ cup of plain barley (not pearled)
2nd four weeks:
8 cups of light brown sugar
Washing the thornapples is not necessary if they were found in a dust-free spot. However, if they are dusty, rinse quickly in cold running water. Drain on several thicknesses of toweling. Chop the thornapples, a few at a time, to the consistency of coleslaw. Put into canner kettle along with the raisins and barley. Add 4 quarts of water, and set in a warm place to ferment for four weeks. Stir and mash the fruit

against the sides of the canner kettle every day during this period.

At the end of the four weeks, strain the fruit through jelly bag, squeezing well to extract all of the juice. Reserve 2 cups of the liquid, and return the rest to canner kettle. Put the sugar into a saucepan with the 2 cups of liquid over a low flame. Stir to prevent any scorching, and when all the sugar is dissolved and while the liquid is still hot, return to canner kettle. Again place in a warm corner to ferment for three additional weeks.

Then strain through several thicknesses of cheesecloth. Siphon immediately into clean sterilized bottles, and cork lightly. When fermentation has ceased, cork tightly and seal with paraffin. Keep for at least six months. Do not open the wine while the thornapple bushes are in bloom. Like the grape, the wine goes through a mild fermentation and may be slightly turbid.

RED THORNAPPLE WINE

1st two weeks:
4 quarts of thornapples
4 quarts of water
2nd two weeks:
8 cups of cane sugar
2 quarts of black raspberries, *or*
2 #2 cans of canned black raspberries
1 package of dry granulated yeast

Chop thornapples as fine as coleslaw. Put into canner kettle along with 4 quarts of water. Set in a warm place to ferment for two weeks. Stir and mash the fruit against the sides of the kettle every day.

At the end of this two-week period, strain through jelly bag, squeezing well to extract all of the liquid. Return to canner kettle and add the well-mashed black raspberries, or canned raspberries. Dissolve the sugar in 2 cups of the liquid over a low flame, stirring so that there is no scorching. While still hot, add to the thornapple-raspberry mixture. Stir well, so that the sugar is distributed evenly. Sprinkle the dry granulated yeast over the surface. Set in a warm place to ferment for two weeks more.

At the end of this period, strain again through jelly bag, squeezing well to extract all of the liquid. Return to canner kettle to settle for two days more. Siphon off into clean sterilized bottles and cork lightly. When fermentation has ceased, cork tightly and seal with paraffin. Keep for at least six months.

HEAVY GOLDEN THORNAPPLE WINE

1st two weeks:
4 quarts of thornapples
1 quart of dried apricots (or two pounds) soaked overnight in water to cover
2 cups of muscat raisins, finely chopped
4 quarts of water
2nd two weeks:
8 cups of cane sugar
3 shredded wheat biscuits *or* 1 cup Wheat Chex

Soak apricots and then bring to a boil in the same water in which they were soaked. Boil slowly for 30 minutes. Stir frequently, since any scorching will alter the flavor of the wine. Set aside to cool to lukewarm.

Meanwhile, chop the thornapples as fine as coleslaw, and put into canner kettle. Add chopped raisins and water. When the apricots have cooled to lukewarm, stir them in also. Set in a warm place to ferment for two weeks. Stir every day, mashing the fruit against the sides of the canner kettle to break it up.

At the end of this period, strain through jelly bag, squeezing well to extract all of the liquid. Return liquid to canner kettle and stir in the sugar, making sure it is all dissolved. If you are using shredded wheat, break it up and sprinkle over the surface. If you are using Wheat Chex, put them over the surface just as they come from the box. Set in a warm place again to ferment for three weeks. No stirring is necessary during this period.

After these three weeks, strain through several thicknesses of cheesecloth and return to canner kettle to settle for two days more. After the settling period, siphon into clean sterilized bottles and cork lightly. Watch this wine closely in the bottle; do not cork too soon. Be sure there are no bubbles of fermentation on the sides. When you are positive, cork tightly, and seal with paraffin. Keep for at least eight months if you're impatient, but a year makes a finer wine.

THORNAPPLE-AND-PLUM WINE

4 quarts of thornapples
2 quarts of Italian plums or damsons (very ripe)
4 quarts of water
8 cups of cane sugar

Pinch each plum between the thumb and forefinger to break the skin. Put into canner kettle. Chop thornapples as fine as coleslaw and add to the plums. Dissolve the sugar in 2 quarts of the water and bring to a boil. While still boiling hot, pour over the plum-thornapple mixture. This hot water and sugar will set the deep red color of the plum skins. Add the remaining 2 quarts of water and set aside to ferment for two weeks. Stir and mash the fruit every day. Be careful not to break any of the plum stones, as this will give a bitter taste to the wine. If you accidently break one open, do your best to get it out of the mash.

At the end of this two-week period, strain through jelly bag, squeezing well to extract all of the juice possible. Return to canner kettle and let stand undisturbed for two weeks more.

At the end of this time (this is four weeks in all, so far), strain through several thicknesses of cheesecloth. Siphon off immediately into clean sterilized bottles. Cork loosely until fermentation has ceased; then cork tightly and seal with paraffin. Keep for six months.

THORNAPPLE-AND-TOKAY-GRAPE WINE
(Light, golden, super-wonderful)

4 quarts of thornapples
2 quarts of Tokay grapes
4 quarts of water
8 cups of cane sugar
1 package of dry granulated yeast (added after two weeks)

Chop thornapples as fine as coleslaw and put into canner kettle. In a separate bowl, crush the Tokay grapes (minus stems) until all grapes are broken. Combine with thornapples. Add the water and stir in the sugar, making sure all is dissolved. Let ferment for two weeks. Stir every day; crush the fruit against the sides of the kettle to break up, and invert the mash every time you stir.

At the end of two weeks, strain through jelly bag, squeezing as dry as possible. Return to canner kettle and sprinkle the dry yeast over the surface. Place in a warm corner to ferment for two weeks more.

After this fermentation period, strain through several thicknesses of cheesecloth. Return to the canner kettle to settle for two days. Siphon off into clean dry bottles and cork lightly. When fermentation has ceased, cork tightly and seal with paraffin. Keep for six months.

Overripe Tokay grapes are best for this recipe. If any are split open, chances are they have an abundance of yeast cells, due to the breakage. Also, increase the amount of Tokay grapes if there happens to be a bargain in overripe fruit at the market.

The Elderberry

Elderberries, like thornapples, are found in almost all countries of the world. Climate and soil determine the size of the fruit. The elder bush has a long history. In fact, the Egyptians used the hollow pithy stem to make a musical instrument called the *sambuke*, a name coined from the botanical classification of the elder, genus *Sambucus*.

Here in the United States elderberry bushes grow along roadways and in roadside ditches. The elderberry has a strange growing procedure: The moment the blossoms drop from the apple tree, the bush will bloom. This is a good rule of thumb to follow in making elderberry wine. Shortly before apples are ripe on the tree, elderberries are ready to pick. Naturally, the amount of sun and protection from surrounding shrubs has a great deal to do with the ripening. The ripe berry, ready for picking, should be red-black in color.

When gathering elderberries, I have found scissors most useful for snipping in close to the clusters without getting too much fleshy stalk. Too, this leaves the bush in good condition for the next season.

If you find a bush you are not sure is elderberry, send a sample to your State Agricultural Department before you make wine. Beware of poisonous bushes which grow in the same manner as the elderberry.

DEEP RED ELDERBERRY WINE

4 quarts of elderberries, loosely packed
4 quarts of water
8 cups of cane sugar

1 cup of muscat raisins, finely chopped
1 ounce of wet yeast
1 slice of white toast

With scissors, cut away the fleshy stalks of the elderberries. Use only the weblike stems upon which the berries are hanging. There is no need to strip the berries from these fine stems; they add color and flavor to the wine. Put them into the canner kettle along with the 4 quarts of water. Bring to a slow rolling boil for 30 minutes. Let cool to lukewarm.

Then strain through jelly bag, squeezing gently to remove all the juice from the fruit. While still lukewarm, stir in the sugar, making sure it is all dissolved. Add raisins, and stir again to distribute evenly. Moisten the yeast with a few drops of water, and spread on one side of the toast. Float the toast, yeast side down, on the surface of the liquid. Set in a warm place to ferment for two weeks *without disturbing*.

At the end of this period, strain through several thicknesses of cheesecloth and return to canner kettle to settle for two days more. Siphon off into clean sterilized bottles and cork lightly. When fermentation has definitely ceased, cork tightly and seal with paraffin. Keep for one year to develop the fullest flavor.

HEAVY ELDERBERRY WINE

4 quarts of loosely packed elderberries
4 quarts of water
8 cups of cane sugar
2 cups of muscat raisins, finely chopped
3 shredded wheat biscuits *or* 1 cup of Wheat Chex
1 package of dry granulated yeast

With scissors, snip away fleshy stalks of elderberries. Put into canner kettle with 4 quarts of water. Boil for 30 minutes. Let cool to lukewarm.

Then strain through jelly bag, squeezing until the pulp is very dry. Return the juice to canner kettle. Stir in the sugar, making sure it is all dissolved. Add the finely chopped raisins. Break shredded wheat over the surface; or, if using Wheat Chex, sprinkle whole over the surface. Distribute the dry yeast over the surface. Put in a warm place to ferment for three weeks. Stir gently twice a week.

At the end of this period, strain through several thicknesses of cheesecloth. Return to canner kettle to settle for two days more. Siphon off into clean sterilized bottles and cork lightly. When fermentation has ceased, cork tightly and seal with paraffin. Keep for one year.

ELDERBERRY WINE
(Sun-extraction method)

1st three days:
4 quarts of loosely packed elderberries (be sure they are dark ripe)
2 quarts of boiling water
final step:
6 cups of cane sugar
1 cup of chopped muscat raisins

This recipe will yield approximately three quarts of wine. If elderberries are abundant, double or triple the recipe—you will have no regrets.

Remove the fleshiest stems from the elderberries and pack in a gallon-sized clear glass jar—such as that described in "The Equipment Is in Your Kitchen." Bring the 2 quarts of water to a rolling boil. Make sure the jar is warm on the outside by setting it in a pan of warm water, or put a metal spoon in it to prevent breakage. Pour the boiling water over the elderberries. Make a plastic liner for the metal cover, and then put the cover on lightly—with, perhaps, a turn and a half. Set in a sunny place outside for three days, or until all the fruit has risen to the top. The liquid should be bright red in color.

Strain through jelly bag, squeezing as much of the liquid as possible from the berries. Put into the glass jar again and stir in the sugar, making sure it is all dissolved. Add chopped raisins, replace the plastic-lined lid loosely and set in a warm place indoors to continue the fermentation process for three more weeks.

At the end of this period, strain through several thicknesses of cheesecloth. Immediately siphon into clean sterilized bottles. Cork lightly at first. Be sure that there are no little bubbles on the inside of the bottle before fastening the cork tightly. Then seal with paraffin. Keep for one year.

SPICY-WARM ELDERBERRY WINE

4 quarts of elderberries, loosely packed
4 quarts of water

8 cups of cane sugar
1 cup of muscat raisins, finely chopped
¼ lb. of candied ginger, finely chopped
10 to 12 black peppercorns
1 package of dry granulated yeast

With scissors, cut away the fleshiest stalks of the elderberries. Put into canner kettle along with the water and boil for 30 minutes. Set aside to cool to lukewarm.

When lukewarm, strain through jelly bag, squeezing until pulp is very dry. Return the liquid to canner kettle and stir in the cane sugar, making sure all of it is dissolved. Add the chopped raisins, the candied ginger and the peppercorns. Sprinkle the dry granulated yeast over the surface and set aside to ferment for two weeks. Stir and invert the mash every day.

At the end of this period, strain through several thicknesses of cheesecloth and return to the canner kettle to settle for two days more. Siphon into clean dry bottles and cork lightly. When all fermentation has ceased, cork tightly and seal with paraffin. Keep for at least eight months before drinking. This is an excellent warm wine for winter use.

Blueberries

There was a time when the wild blueberry was so abundant that it could be purchased at city markets. Now, due to forest fires, drought, and careless picking, many regions are practically without them. It took the flip of a coin to decide whether or not to include blueberries under this chapter dealing with wild berries. There are domestic blueberries on the market that are real whoppers, but for my taste, they have lost in cultivation a lot of the flavor that the smaller wild variety had.

If you're lucky enough to live near one of those heavenly regions where the blueberry is still abundant, you'll never waste them on muffins or pies again!

BLUEBERRY WINE

4 quarts of wild or domestic blueberries
4 quarts of water
8 cups of cane sugar
1 slice of whole wheat toast
1 ounce of wet yeast

If the woods where you pick the berries are cool and clean, do not wash berries; but if they are gritty and dusty, rinse quickly under cold running water. Then put them into canner kettle, and mash thoroughly with a potato masher. Bring 2 quarts of the water to a boil, along with the sugar. Boil for 5 minutes, then pour over berries. This will set the red-purple color. Add the other 2 quarts of cool water and stir well. Moisten yeast with a few drops of water and spread on the toast. Float the toast, yeast side down, on the surface of the liquid. Put in a warm place to ferment for two weeks. Stir gently from the bottom every day during this period.

Then strain through jelly bag, squeezing pulp very dry to extract all of the color and flavor. Return to canner kettle to settle for two days. Then siphon off into clean sterilized bottles and cork lightly. This wine takes about three weeks to finish fermenting in the bottle, so don't be too eager to fasten the corks tightly. When fermentation has ceased, cork tightly and seal with paraffin. Keep for at least six months; but if you wait a year the body and color of the wine will greatly improve.

BLUEBERRY-CHERRY WINE

1st two weeks:
3 quarts of blueberries
3 quarts of black-ripe Bing cherries
4 quarts of water, room temperature
2nd two weeks:
8 cups of cane sugar
2 large shredded wheat biscuits *or* 1 cup Wheat Chex
1 package of dry granulated yeast

Combine the blueberries and the Bing cherries in the canner kettle and mash with a potato masher until fine. Be careful not to break the cherry pits, as they will give the wine a bitter taste. Add the room-temperature water, and set in a warm place to ferment for two weeks. Stir every day.

At the end of this time, strain through jelly bag, squeezing well to extract all of the flavor and liquid. Reserve 2 cups of liquid for dissolving the sugar; return the rest to the canner kettle. Dissolve the sugar in the two cups of liquid over a low flame; bring to a boil for five minutes. While still hot, add to the liquid in the canner kettle. Crumble the shredded wheat and add; if using Wheat Chex, add them as they come from the box. Stir well to circulate the sugar and the wheat; then sprinkle the dry granulated yeast over the surface. Set in a warm place to ferment for two weeks without disturbing.

At the end of this second two-week period, strain through several thicknesses of cheesecloth and return to the canner kettle to settle for two days more. Siphon off into clean sterilized bottles and cork lightly until fermentation has ceased. When fermentation is over, cork tightly and seal with paraffin. Keep for six months.

A Few Words on Wild Berries Not Listed

Certain regions of the country boast many varieties of delicious wild berries which I have not mentioned here. These berries travel under many local names—June berries, May berries, thimble berries, rambling currants, etc. If there are edible berries growing near your home, they will probably make delicious wine. The first caution, however, is to check them with your State Agricultural Department. Send them a specimen of the berries, along with some of the leaves.

If sending a specimen entails too much time, take samples to the local high school biology department, the biology department of a museum, or to a forest ranger station.

A good basic recipe to follow for wild berries is the one for Black or Red Raspberry Wine included in the next chapter, "Wine from Tame Berries."

Be sure to pick berries when the sun is high in the sky and all dew and moisture are gone. If the picking spot is shady and damp, this rule is still good, for the heat of the sun will have dried them to a great extent. You should observe this rule because dew sometimes provides a resting place for wild yeasts and bacteria which may possibly lead to wine spoilage.

Never attempt to make wine from wild berries of which you are not 100% sure. It costs nothing to have them properly identified, and it is a good safe practice.

CHAPTER VI

Wine from Tame Berries

Botanically speaking, any fruit that has interior seeds is a berry. Therefore, oranges, lemons, apples, grapes, watermelons—even tomatoes—are generally considered as being in the berry class. Oddly enough, this rule excludes strawberries from being classified as berries.

In this chapter I am going to deal with berries as the housewife knows them—for table use, canning and freezing. Since strawberries are a universal favorite, they head the list. If strawberries give you hives, get your quota without the itch—make wine from them!

SWEET STRAWBERRY WINE

- 4 quarts of ripe strawberries (you may even use overripe berries)
- 4 quarts of water
- 8 cups of cane sugar
- 1 lb. of white raisins, finely chopped
- 1 ounce of wet yeast
- 1 slice of white toast

Remove the green stems from the berries and put berries into the canner kettle. Mash very fine with a potato masher. Add the 4 quarts of water and place over a low flame until it comes to a rolling boil. Remove from heat and let cool to lukewarm.

Then strain through jelly bag, squeezing very dry. Reserve 3 cups of liquid to dissolve the sugar. Put the sugar in a saucepan with the 3 cups of liquid over a low flame and stir until sugar is dissolved. Add the sugar mixture and the chopped raisins to the rest of the berries; stir well so that all is thoroughly mixed. Test for temperature by putting a drop on your wrist; it should just feel warm. Moisten yeast with a few drops of water and spread on one side of the toast. Float the toast, yeast side down, on the surface of the liquid. Set in a warm place to ferment for one week. Stir every day.

At the end of this week, strain through several thicknesses of cheesecloth, and return to the canner kettle to settle for two days longer. Then siphon into clean sterilized bottles and cork lightly. When fermentation has ceased, cork tightly and seal with paraffin. To have excellent wine, keep for one year.

STRAWBERRY-CHERRY WINE

4 quarts of very ripe strawberries
4 quarts of tart pie cherries
8 cups of cane sugar
2 shredded wheat biscuits *or* 1 cup whole Wheat Chex
4 quarts of tepid water
1 package of dry granulated yeast

This wine takes as much care as a six-month-old baby but, like a baby, it's well worth the trouble.

Put the hulled strawberries into a canner kettle and mash well with potato masher. Pinch each cherry between forefinger and thumb to break the skin, but leave the pit in; add to the strawberries. Add the crumbled shredded wheat or the Wheat Chex (as they come from the box). Add the room-temperature water; mix all very well by stirring for several minutes. Then stir in the sugar, making sure all is dissolved. Sprinkle the dry yeast over the surface. Set in a warm place to ferment for three weeks. This is where the extra-special care comes in: The mash must be stirred three times a day! A good rule is to stir it after breakfast, lunch, and dinner. This wine is prone to form a greenish mold; remove any sign of it immediately with a slotted spoon.

At the end of the three-week period, strain through jelly bag, squeezing pulp very dry to extract all the juice and flavor. Immediately siphon into clean, sterilized bottles. I always put in about one inch of artists' charcoal sketching stick, which will combat any mustiness from the mold. This charcoal trick is described in the chapter "The Spirit Is Willing If—" When you are absolutely sure fermentation is over, cork tightly and seal with paraffin. Keep for six months.

BLACK OR RED RASPBERRY WINE

(This recipe is for either wild or tame berries)

1st day:
4 quarts of black or red raspberries
2 quarts of water
2nd day:

2 quarts of water

6 cups of cane sugar (if you prefer a sweet wine, increase
   sugar to 8 cups)

Gather berries on a bright day after dew has evaporated.
If purchasing berries, rest assured they were picked under
these conditions. Most commercial berry growers pick only
sun-dried fruit, because it keeps much better in the stores.
Remove all stems and any green centers which may be in the
shell of the berry meat.

Put berries into canner kettle and crush with potato masher.
Bring 2 quarts of water to a rapid boil and pour over the
crushed berries. This will set the color. Stir well, and set in a
warm place until the next day.

The following day, dissolve the sugar in the remaining 2
quarts of water over a low flame. Set aside to cool to lukewarm. When lukewarm, stir into the berry mixture so that
the sugar is distributed evenly. Set in a warm place to ferment for two weeks. Stir every day, crushing the fruit against
the sides of the canner kettle; also invert berries which have
come to the top.

At the end of this period, strain through jelly bag, squeezing quite dry. Return to canner kettle to settle for two days
longer. Siphon off into clean sterilized bottles and cork lightly.
When fermentation has ceased, cork tightly and seal with
paraffin. Keep for at least six months. If kept a year, this will
develop the body and flavor of raspberry liqueur.

CHERRY WINE

1st two days:

4 quarts of tart red cherries

2 quarts of water

2nd stage:

2 quarts of water

1 cup of white raisins, finely chopped

1 slice of white toast

1 ounce of wet yeast

8 cups sugar

Pick over cherries, making sure there are no pieces of
stems. If the trees were sprayed after the crop was ripe,
rinse cherries in cold running water and drain on several
thicknesses of toweling. If buying the cherries, washing is a
must, for cultivated cherries have almost always been sprayed.
If you know positively that the tree was not sprayed, washing

is not desirable, as it will decrease the number of active wine yeast cells.

Pinch each cherry between thumb and forefinger so that the skin is well broken. Bring 2 quarts of the water to a rapid boil and pour over the cherries. Set aside in a warm place for two days. Then dissolve the sugar in the remaining 2 quarts of water over a low flame. While still hot, add to the cherry mixture. Add the finely chopped raisins. Moisten the yeast with a few drops of water, and spread on one side of the toast. Float the toast, yeast side down, on the surface of the liquid. Let stand for two weeks. Stir every day, crushing the fruit against the sides of the canner kettle to break it up. Try not to break any of the pits, as the nutlike center will give bitterness to the wine.

At the end of the fermentation period, strain through jelly bag, squeezing as dry as possible. Return the liquid to the canner kettle and let stand undisturbed for two weeks longer. Then taste the wine, and if it is too tart, add sugar.

At the end of this second two-week period, strain through several thicknesses of cheesecloth and return to the canner kettle to settle for two days longer. Siphon into clean sterilized bottles and cork lightly. If you have added extra sugar, watch wine closely, for there will be a longer fermentation period in the bottle. When wine is through fermenting, cork tightly and seal with paraffin.

The tart red cherry does not give a deep red wine. If the name "Cherry Wine" conjures up a vision of a much deeper red, add about 1 tablespoon of red food coloring just before the settling period.

BING CHERRY WINE
(Dark red, delicious)

1st day:
- 4 quarts of very ripe Bing cherries (they can even be over-ripe)
- 2 quarts of water

2nd day:
- 2 quarts of water
- 8 cups of cane sugar
- 1 cup of muscat raisins, finely chopped
- 1 slice of whole wheat toast
- 1 ounce of wet yeast

If cherries have not been sprayed, no washing is necessary.

If there is any doubt, wash in cold running water. Put cherries into canner kettle and mash very gently with potato masher. Be careful not to crack open the stones, or the wine will have a bitter taste. However, do not remove the stones, for in their whole condition they add flavor. Bring 2 quarts of water to a rapid boil and pour over the cherries. This will set their dark red color. Put aside overnight in a warm place.

The following day, dissolve sugar in the remaining 2 quarts of water over a low flame. While still hot, stir into cherry-water mixture. Add finely chopped raisins. Moisten the yeast with a few drops of water, and spread on one side of the whole wheat toast. Float the toast, yeast side down, on surface of liquid. Put in a warm place to ferment for two weeks.

At the end of this period, strain through jelly bag, squeezing the pulp as dry as possible. Return the liquid to the canner kettle and let stand undisturbed for two weeks longer.

Then strain through several thicknesses of cheesecloth and return to the canner kettle to settle for two days more. At the end of the settling period, siphon off into clean sterilized bottles and cork lightly. When the fermentation has ceased, cork tightly and seal with paraffin. Keep for six months.

Avoid opening this wine when the cherry blossoms are on the tree, for it goes through a period of light fermentation at this time and the wine will have a sharp flavor and be turbid instead of clear.

Currants

Making wine from currants is a very old practice. There is a basically sound reason why the currant was recognized early as a winemaker. Like the grape, the currant has quantities of natural wine yeast cells on its skin. As a rule, currants are seldom sprayed, so washing isn't too essential. Besides, if they aren't washed, more yeast cells will be present to start the fermentation.

If there are currant bushes in your own yard, pick the currants in the heat of the afternoon when all dew and moisture have been dried off by the sun. Rest assured those on the market were picked under the same conditions; every farmer's wife knows that currants picked in the morning dew will mold in the box.

RED CURRANT WINE

4 quarts of red currants (be sure they are ripe)
4 quarts of water
8 cups of cane sugar

Put 2 quarts of currants into the canner kettle and crush with a potato masher. Place the other 2 quarts into a large mixing bowl and crush.

Dissolve the sugar in 2 quarts of the water. Place over a low flame; stir well, so that there will be no scorching. Bring to a rolling boil. Pour this boiling sugar-water over the currants in canner kettle. Set aside to cool to lukewarm.

Then add the other 2 quarts of crushed currants, and the remaining 2 quarts of water. I find that preparing this recipe in this manner preserves the natural yeast cells present and starts a quicker and much sounder fermentation. The boiling water over the first half of the currants extracts the beautiful red color and fixes it. If only cold water were used on the currants all the way through, the wine eventually produced would be very pale instead of a robust red. Set the mixture aside to ferment for one week. Stir well every day.

At the end of this week, strain through jelly bag, squeezing quite dry. Then return the liquid to canner kettle and allow to ferment for two weeks without disturbing.

Then strain through several thicknesses of cheesecloth and immediately siphon into clean sterilized bottles. Cork lightly, and when fermentation has ceased, cork tightly and seal with paraffin. Keep this wine for at least eighteen months—a year and a half. This is one of the most delicious of homemade wines when properly aged, but it requires patience!

STRONG RED-AND-WHITE CURRANT WINE

4 quarts of red currants
4 quarts of white currants
4 quarts of water
8 cups of cane sugar

Put the currants into canner kettle and crush thoroughly with a potato masher. Bring 1 quart of the water to a rapid boil, and add the sugar; boil for a few seconds longer. Stir this boiling-hot mixture into the two kinds of crushed currants. This will set a delicate red color into the wine—the white currants, of course, contribute no color. Let stand until lukewarm, and then add the 3 remaining quarts of cool water. Set in a warm place to ferment for one week. Stir every day, crushing the fruit against the sides of the canner kettle. Be sure to invert the mash each time you stir.

At the end of this week, strain through jelly bag, squeezing very well so that all the liquid and flavor are extracted. Return the liquid to your canner kettle to ferment for two weeks longer. No stirring is necessary in this last fermentation period.

At the end of this period (this makes three weeks' fermentation in all), strain through several thicknesses of cheesecloth and siphon into clean sterilized bottles. Cork lightly at first, and when fermentation is over, cork tightly and seal with paraffin. This, like most currant wines, must age for eighteen months.

PALE GOLD GOOSEBERRY WINE

4 quarts of yellow gooseberries, with heads and tails removed
4 quarts of water
2 cups of white raisins, finely chopped
3 shredded wheat biscuits, or 1½ cups of Wheat Chex
8 cups of cane sugar
1 package of dry granulated yeast

Mash gooseberries with potato masher, breaking up the fruit as much as possible. Stir in the chopped raisins. Break up the shredded wheat biscuits and stir into the fruit. When using Wheat Chex, add just as they come from the box. Dissolve the sugar in 2 quarts of the water over a low flame, and bring to a rolling boil. While waiting for the sugar and water to boil, add the 2 remaining quarts of cool water to the gooseberries and raisins. Then stir in the boiling sugar-water. Test a drop on your arm to see if it is lukewarm, and then sprinkle the dry granulated yeast over the surface. Set in a warm place to ferment for two weeks. Stir every day, mashing and inverting the fruit.

At the end of the two-week period, strain through jelly bag, squeezing very dry to extract all the liquid and flavor. Return the liquid to canner kettle for two additional weeks of fermentation. Do not disturb during this second fermenting period.

Then strain through several thicknesses of cheesecloth;

siphon immediately into clean sterilized bottles and cork lightly. When fermentation has ceased, cork tightly and seal with paraffin.

Gooseberry wines have a tendency to develop a bottom cloud. If this is siphoned into the bottles, it seems to take forever to clear. A good way to overcome this is to place a piece of absorbent sterile cotton about the size of an egg in the funnel. This will act as a very efficient filter and catch many of the solids which cause the cloud. If cotton becomes saturated with solids during the siphoning, use a new piece.

RED CURRANT-RASPBERRY WINE

3 quarts of red currants
2 quarts of red raspberries *or* 2 #2 cans red raspberries
4 quarts of water (2 quarts to be added next day)
8 cups of sugar

Pick over currants, heading and tailing them. Put them into canner kettle and crush with potato masher. Dissolve the sugar in 2 quarts of the water over a low flame. Bring to a rolling boil, and while still hot pour over the currants. In another bowl crush the raspberries and then stir into water-currant mixture. Let stand overnight.

The following day, add the 2 remaining quarts of cool water; mix well, and set in a warm place to ferment for two weeks.

At the end of this period, strain through jelly bag, squeezing well to extract all of the liquid. Return to the canner kettle for one week more of fermentation.

Strain through several thicknesses of cheesecloth, and siphon immediately into clean sterilized bottles. Cork lightly for the first two weeks. When fermentation in the bottle has definitely ceased, cork tightly and seal with paraffin. This wine should be kept for at least a year.

FORTIFIED GOOSEBERRY WINE

1st day:
4 quarts of green gooseberries
8 cups of sugar
2nd day:
4 quarts of warm water
1 package of dry granulated yeast

3rd step:

1 cup of imported gin

Pick over the gooseberries; remove heads or tails. Put into canner kettle and mash well with a potato masher. Cover with the sugar and set aside overnight.

The following day, add the warm water, stirring well to dissolve any of the sugar which may not have turned to syrup. Sprinkle the dry yeast over the surface and set in a warm place to ferment for one week. Stir every day, inverting any fruit which may rise to the surface.

At the end of this week, strain through jelly bag, squeezing very dry. Add the cup of gin and set in a warm place to ferment for one week more.

At the end of the second week (this makes only two weeks' fermentation in all), strain through several thicknesses of cheesecloth. Siphon immediately into clean sterilized bottles and cork lightly.

Leave the bottles lightly corked for at least two weeks, since this wine does quite a bit of active fermenting in the bottle. When fermentation is over, tap each bottle to make sure there are no bubbles running up the sides. Then cork tightly and seal with paraffin. Keep for at least six months.

The gin is purely optional. However, we have tried making this wine both ways and definitely have found the fortified wine better in clearing, color, and flavor.

CRANBERRY WINE

Tired of serving the traditional cranberry sauce with Thanksgiving turkey? Try drinking homemade Cranberry Wine instead. It can be made late in winter, while cranberries are still available, and served the following Thanksgiving.

4 quarts of cranberries
4 quarts of water
8 cups of cane sugar

Chop cranberries a cup at a time and put them into canner kettle. Dissolve sugar in 2 quarts of the water over a low flame; when dissolved, bring to a boil for 5 minutes. While still boiling hot, pour over the chopped cranberries. Add the remaining 2 quarts of cool water. Set in a warm place to ferment for two weeks. Stir every day, inverting any fruit which rises to the top.

After the two-week period, strain through jelly bag, squeezing as dry as possible. Return to the canner kettle to settle for one additional week.

At the end of this settling period, siphon off into clean sterilized bottles. This wine has a tendency to work for some time, so cork lightly. Be sure fermentation has ceased before corking tightly; then seal with paraffin. Keep for ten months for best flavor.

DEEP RED CRANBERRY WINE

1st day:
- 4 quarts of cranberries
- 2 #2 cans of black raspberries
- 2 quarts of water

2nd day:
- 2 quarts of water

3rd step:
- 8 cups of cane sugar
- 4 cups of muscat raisins, finely chopped
- 1 ounce of wet yeast
- 1 slice of whole wheat toast

Chop cranberries a cup at a time until they are quite fine. Put the cranberries and the black raspberries into canner kettle. Bring 2 quarts of the water to a boil and pour over cranberries and raspberries. Let stand overnight. The following day, add the 2 remaining quarts of water. Set in a warm place to ferment for one week. Stir every day, completely turning the mash.

At the end of the week, strain through jelly bag, squeezing well so that all the juice is extracted from the pulp. Return the juice to canner kettle and add the chopped raisins. Add the sugar and stir well so that all is dissolved. Moisten the yeast with a few drops of water and spread on one side of the whole wheat toast. Float the toast, yeast side down, on the surface of the liquid. Set in a warm place to ferment for two weeks longer. Stir daily, lifting from the bottom. Try not to break up the toast in the stirring process.

At the end of this two-week period, strain through jelly bag, squeezing lightly. Return to canner kettle to settle for two days more. Siphon into clean sterilized bottles and cork lightly. When fermentation is over, cork tightly and seal with paraffin. Keep for ten months. This is a rich, heavy-bodied wine which goes very well with meat courses.

MULBERRY WINE (Fortified)

1st two days:
4 quarts of mulberries
4 quarts of boiling water
2nd step:
8 cups of sugar
1 crushed eggshell
8 to 10 cassia buds
1 package of dry granulated yeast
3rd step:
1 cup of domestic grape brandy

Avoid washing the mulberries if possible, but if they are dusty and gritty, rinse them quickly in cold running water. Put the berries into canner kettle and crush with potato masher. Pour over them 4 quarts of boiling water. This will set their delicate red color. Let stand for two days.

Then strain through jelly bag, squeezing the pulp as dry as possible. Return the juice to canner kettle and stir in the sugar. Stir well from the bottom so that all the sugar is dissolved. Sprinkle in the crushed eggshell, which will give the wine clearness. Add the cassia buds; with their delicate cinnamon flavor, they will give this wine a little more character. Sprinkle the dry granulated yeast over the surface. Set aside to ferment for one week. Stir every day.

At the end of this week, strain through several thicknesses of cheesecloth. Add the cup of brandy, and set aside to settle for one week more. Then siphon into clean sterilized bottles and cork lightly. When fermentation has ceased, cork tightly and seal with paraffin. Keep for at least one year.

The addition of the cup of brandy gives a lot to this wine; it heightens flavor and greatly increases fermentation.

Dried Berries

Raisins, figs, and dates are berries, theoretically. So I am including these recipes in the tame berry group. Dried fruits of any kind are marvelous winemakers. The yeast cells remain active because they are suspended in about a 10% moisture content, just as the major yeast companies suspend their yeast cells in a "dry" state for dry granulated yeast. With the addition of water, the cells take up growing and multiplying again just where they left off before their enforced hibernation period.

Other dried fruits, such as apricots, peaches and prunes, are dealt with in the chapter "Wine from Everyday Fruits," which immediately follows this one.

NIPPY LIGHT RAISIN WINE

3 lbs. of white raisins, finely chopped
1/4 lb. of candied ginger, finely chopped
1 lb. of cracked wheat
8 cups of cane sugar
1 lemon cut into 1/4" slices
1 orange cut into 1/4" slices
1 package of dry granulated yeast
4 quarts of room-temperature water

Put the raisins, ginger, wheat, lemons and oranges into canner kettle. Add all of the water except 3 cups. Put the sugar into a saucepan with the 3 cups of water and dissolve over a low flame. Then add the sugar-water to the first mixture. Sprinkle the dry granulated yeast over the surface. Put in a warm place to ferment for four weeks. Stir every day. Push to the bottom any of the fruit which rises.

At the end of the four weeks, strain through jelly bag; return to the canner kettle to settle for one week. Siphon into clean sterilized bottles and cork lightly until all fermentation has ceased. Then cork tightly and seal with paraffin. Age for at least five months.

This is a fine light wine that can be made at any time of the year. It so closely resembles light sherry that we've stumped many of our friends.

HEAVY RAISIN WINE

6 cups of muscat raisins, finely chopped
2 lemons cut into 1/4" slices
2 oranges cut into 1/4" slices
4 quarts of water
3 level tablespoons of instant black tea
10 cups of cane sugar
3 shredded wheat biscuits *or* 1 1/2 cups of Wheat Chex
1 ounce of dry granulated yeast

Chop the raisins very fine; in this instance, as there is a considerable amount, the task is easier if they are put through a food grinder, using the coarse blade. Put into a large mixing bowl. Add sliced lemons and oranges, and the shredded wheat broken up into fine pieces, or the Wheat Chex just as they come from the box. Mix all together very well, and set aside.

Put the 4 quarts of water into canner kettle, along with the sugar. Set over a low flame and stir until all the sugar is dissolved. Then bring to a rolling boil. Mix the instant black tea with enough water to make a thin, smooth paste. Remove the sugar-water from the fire and stir in the dissolved instant tea. Cool to lukewarm.

Then add fruit mixture. Stir all very well. Sprinkle dry granulated yeast over the surface. Set in a warm place to ferment for three weeks. Stir daily, inverting any fruit which may rise to the top.

At the end of this three-week period, strain through jelly bag, squeezing well to remove all of the liquid. Return to canner kettle to settle for two days longer. Siphon into clean sterilized bottles and cork lightly. This wine does a great deal of working in the bottle, so watch carefully for signs of fermentation before final corking. Tap each bottle lightly, and if no fine bubbles appear on the inside, cork tightly and seal with paraffin. Keep for six months.

This wine has fooled many of our friends; they think they are drinking heavy imported sherry. Try it on your guests; they'll never believe you made it in your own kitchen.

DRIED FIG WINE

1st day:
8 cups of dried figs, either light or dark variety; approximately four lbs.
3 cups of muscat raisins, finely chopped
2 quarts of water
2nd day:
2 quarts of water
6 cups of cane sugar
1 package of dry granulated yeast

Chop the figs to the consistency of coleslaw, or put through food grinder, using coarse blade. Add chopped raisins and stir in 2 quarts of cold water. Set aside overnight.

The following day, dissolve 6 cups of sugar in the remaining 2 quarts of water over a low flame. While still hot, add to the fig-raisin mixture. Mix well and set in a warm place to ferment for two weeks. Stir well every day, and invert the mash; figs and raisins have a habit of rising to the top and forming a crust.

At the end of this two-week period, strain through jelly bag, squeezing very dry to extract all the liquid and flavor. Return to canner kettle and sprinkle the dry granulated yeast over the surface. Let stand for two more weeks without disturbing.

Then strain through several thicknesses of cheesecloth. If necessary, strain twice; fig seeds are tiny, and if any are left in the wine it will take longer to clear. Return to canner kettle to settle for two days more.

At the end of the settling period, siphon into clean sterilized bottles and cork lightly. When fermentation is over, cork tightly and seal with paraffin. Keep for at least six months.

FRESH FIG WINE

1st day:
3 quarts of fresh ripe figs, either light or dark
2 quarts of water
2nd day:
2 quarts of water
6 cups of cane sugar
1 cup of raisins, finely chopped (If using light figs, use light raisins.)

If you're in a region of the United States where fig trees flourish, you can make a wonderful wine. Wine from fresh figs dates back to ancient Persia.

Avoid washing the figs if possible; but if they are gritty or dusty, or have been sprayed, then washing is necessary. Use cold running water, and drain on several thicknesses of toweling. Chop the figs quite fine with food chopper and put into canner kettle. Cover with 2 quarts of cold water, and let stand overnight.

The following day, dissolve the sugar in the remaining 2 quarts of water over a low flame. While still hot, add chopped figs and water in canner kettle. Add the finely chopped raisins and stir well. Set in a warm place to ferment for two weeks. Stir every day, mashing the fruit and pushing to the bottom any that rises.

At the end of this two-week period, strain through jelly

bag and return to the canner kettle. Let stand for two weeks more without disturbing.

Then strain through several thicknesses of cheesecloth to eliminate seeds. Put back into canner kettle to settle for two days more. Siphon into clean sterilized bottles and cork lightly until fermentation stops. When there are no further signs of fermentation, cork tightly and seal with paraffin. Keep for six months.

DATE WINE

1st day:

8 cups of dates (with the pits in; always cheaper, and pits add flavor)

2 quarts of water

2nd day:

6 cups of cane sugar

3 lemons cut into 1/4" slices

2 quarts of water

1 package of dry granulated yeast

Cut dates lengthwise to expose the stones. Put into canner kettle with 2 quarts of water. Set aside overnight. The following day, dissolve the sugar over a low flame in the 2 remaining quarts of water. Bring to a boil, and while still hot add to dates and water in canner kettle. Add the sliced lemons, and sprinkle the dry granulated yeast over the surface. Set in a warm place to ferment for two weeks. Stir every day, mashing up dates as much as possible during this stirring period.

Then strain through jelly bag, squeezing the pulp very dry. Return to canner kettle for two more weeks of fermentation. Do not disturb in this second fermentation period.

Strain through several thicknesses of cheesecloth and siphon immediately into clean sterilized bottles. Cork lightly until fermentation has ceased. Tap each bottle for signs of small bubbles running up the sides. Seal tightly and dip in paraffin. Keep this wine for at least five months.

Date wine is on the sweet side, and goes wonderfully with desserts. Try adding a tumblerful of this wine to fruit cocktail—an excellent dessert with a new flavor!

CHAPTER VII

Wine from Everyday Fruits

The Apple of Your Eye....

There is the old bromide about an apple a day keeping away the doctor. Yet to be proved is whether or not a glass of apple wine per day will produce the same results. No matter what's decided in the future, apple wine will remain an American favorite. Wines and ciders from apples have been with us for centuries, but here we are going to deal only with apple wines. Many of the recipes which follow are very old, but have been put into modern measurements for your convenience.

Apples, thanks to Johnny Appleseed, grow abundantly almost everywhere in the United States. Some states excel as apple-growing regions, producing fruit of exceptional size and quality. Whether or not you live in an apple state makes little difference; almost any apple, whether it is a picture of beauty or an average homegrown one, will make excellent wine.

GOLDEN APPLE WINE

1st four weeks:
10 lbs. of apples (windfalls are wonderful for this wine)
2 cups of muscat raisins, finely chopped
1 cup of barley (not pearled)
4 quarts of water
Last stage:
6 cups of light brown sugar
If using windfalls, any brown spots and bruises should be left on the apples, as they speed fermentation. Cut apples in quarters to make chopping easier, and then chop as fine as coleslaw. Put into canner kettle with the raisins and barley. Add water; stir well. Put in a warm place to ferment for four weeks. Stir well every day.

At the end of four weeks' time, strain through jelly bag,

squeezing well. Return to canner kettle and stir in the light brown sugar. Make sure it all dissolves. Set in a warm place to ferment for an additional three weeks. No stirring is necessary during this period.

At the end of this three weeks (that makes seven weeks in all), strain through several thicknesses of cheesecloth. Siphon immediately into clean, dry bottles and cork lightly. When fermentation has ceased, and there are no bubbles running up the inside of the bottles, cork tightly and seal with paraffin. This wine should age at least six months in the bottle. At the end of a year, it will take on a heavier body and a richer color.

DEEP AMBER APPLE WINE

1st two weeks:
- 8 lbs. of apples, any variety
- 4 quarts of water
- 8 cups of dried apricots, soaked overnight in 2 quarts of water
- 2 cups of unpitted dates

Next step:
- 2 cups of muscat raisins, finely chopped
- 1 large shredded wheat biscuit, *or* 1 cup of Wheat Chex
- 8 cups of cane sugar
- 12 peppercorns

While chopping up the apples, put soaked apricots along with the 2 quarts of water over a low flame. Bring to a gentle boil for about 30 minutes. Stir from time to time to prevent scorching. When the apricots are tender enough to break with a fork, set aside to cool to lukewarm. Then add the chopped apples and the remaining 2 quarts of water. Set in a warm place to ferment for two weeks. Stir every day, inverting the fruit and mashing well.

At the end of this two-week period, strain through jelly bag, squeezing very well. Return to canner kettle. Split open the dates with a sharp knife to expose the stones, and add to the liquid. Add the finely chopped raisins. Crumble and add the shredded wheat; if you are using Wheat Chex, add as they are. Stir in the sugar and add peppercorns. Set in a warm place for three more weeks of fermentation. No stirring is necessary during this period.

Then strain again through jelly bag, squeezing pulp as

dry as possible. Immediately siphon into clean, sterilized bottles and cork lightly. When fermentation has definitely ceased, cork tightly and seal with paraffin. Keep for six months.

APPLE-AND-BLACK RASPBERRY WINE

6 lbs. of apples, any variety
3 quarts of fresh black raspberries or 3 #2 cans black raspberries
2 cups of muscat raisins
3 quarts of water
8 cups of cane sugar (add after two weeks)

Quarter and chop apples as fine as coleslaw. Put into canner kettle with 3 quarts of water. Crush raspberries with a potato masher and add them and the raisins to apples. If using canned berries, add just as they come from the can. Set in a warm place to ferment for two weeks. Stir well every day.

At the end of the two weeks, strain through jelly bag, squeezing very dry to extract all of the liquid. Return to canner kettle and stir in the sugar, making absolutely sure all of it is dissolved. Put in a warm place to ferment for another two weeks.

Then strain through several thicknesses of cheesecloth, and return to canner kettle to settle for two days longer. Siphon into clean sterilized bottles and cork lightly. Tap each bottle for signs of fermentation before final sealing. Fasten the corks tightly and seal with paraffin. This wine should be kept for one year. In that length of time, it will develop a fine flavor and a very deep red color.

SCARLET APPLE WINE

6 lbs. of apples, any variety
4 lbs. of red beets
8 cups of cane sugar
3 cups of muscat raisins, finely chopped
4 quarts of water
1 package of dry granulated yeast

First scrub the beets well, removing stems and tails. Cut into quarters for easier chopping, and then chop them to coleslaw consistency. Put the chopped beets into canner kettle along with 4 quarts of water, and bring to a boil for 30 minutes. Set aside to cool to lukewarm.

While beet liquid is cooling, quarter and chop the apples as fine as coleslaw. Then strain the beet liquid through jelly bag, squeezing as dry as possible. Return liquid to canner kettle and stir in the sugar, making sure all is dissolved. Add chopped apples and raisins and mix very well. Then sprinkle dry granulated yeast over the surface. Set in a warm place to ferment for two weeks. Stir every day, inverting the mash.

At the end of this two-week period, strain through jelly bag, squeezing quite dry. Siphon immediately into clean sterilized bottles and cork lightly. Before fastening the corks tightly and sealing with paraffin, check for signs of fermentation by tapping each bottle. If there are bubbles running up the sides the wine is still fermenting and is not ready for permanent corking. Keep this wine for six months.

APPLE-CRANBERRY WINE

1st week:
  6 lbs. of apples, any tart variety
  8 cups of cranberries
  4 quarts of water
2nd week:
  8 cups of cane sugar
  1 slice of whole wheat toast
  1 ounce of wet yeast
  2 cups of muscat raisins

Chop the cranberries very fine and put into canner kettle. Pour 2 quarts of boiling water over them. This will set the red color of the wine. Set aside to cool. Chop the apples up very fine and add to the cranberries along with the remaining 2 quarts of water. Put in a warm place to ferment for one week.

Then strain through jelly bag, squeezing very dry. Return to canner kettle and add the sugar; stir well, so that it is all dissolved. Add the chopped raisins. Moisten the yeast with a few drops of water, and spread on one side of the toast. Float the toast, yeast side down, on the surface of the liquid. Set in a warm place to ferment for two more weeks. Stir twice a week.

At the end of this two-week period, strain again through

jelly bag, squeezing quite dry. Return to canner kettle to settle for two days longer. Then siphon off into clean sterilized bottles and cork lightly until fermentation ceases. After the wine has stopped all of its activity, cork tightly and seal with paraffin. Keep for at least four months.

APPLE-CURRANT WINE

4 lbs. of apples
4 lbs. of dried currants (zante)
6 cups of cane sugar
2 cups of cracked wheat
1 package of dry granulated yeast
4 quarts of water

Soak currants overnight in 4 quarts of water. The next day bring them to a boil in same water and boil for an hour. Set aside to cool to lukewarm. While cooling, chop apples to the consistency of coleslaw. Add apples, cracked wheat, and the sugar to the currant juice. Stir very well so that all of the sugar is dissolved. Sprinkle the dry granulated yeast over the surface and set in a warm place to ferment for three weeks. Stir every day during this period, crushing the fruit against the sides of the canner kettle.

At the end of this three-week period, strain through jelly bag, squeezing very dry. Return to canner kettle to settle for three days more. Then siphon into clean sterilized bottles and cork lightly. When fermentation has ceased, cork tightly and seal with paraffin.

This wine should be kept for one year before opening—during which time it will develop amazing flavor and a deep topaz color.

APPLE-PEAR WINE

3 lbs. of windfall apples
3 lbs. of very ripe Bartlett pears
2 cups of muscat raisins, finely chopped
8 cups of cane sugar
4 quarts of water
1 large shredded wheat biscuit, *or* 1 cup of Wheat Chex
1 package of dry granulated yeast

Ignore any brown spots on the apples and pears, as they will aid fermentation. Cut in quarters, then chop as fine as possible. Put into canner kettle along with chopped raisins, crumbled shredded wheat or whole Wheat Chex. Dissolve sugar in 2 quarts of the water over a long flame; set aside to cool to lukewarm. Add the sugar-water and the remaining 2 quarts of cool water. Stir all very well. Sprinkle the dry granulated yeast over the surface. Set in a warm place to ferment for two weeks.

Then strain through jelly bag, squeezing quite dry, and return to canner kettle for two more weeks of fermentation. No stirring is necessary during this period.

At the end of this second fermentation period, strain through several thicknesses of cheesecloth and immediately siphon into clean sterilized bottles. Cork lightly until fermentation stops, and then fasten the corks tightly and seal with paraffin. Keep for at least six months.

APPLE-FIG WINE

4 lbs. of tart apples
8 cups of dried black figs
2 cups of seedless raisins
8 cups of cane sugar
4 quarts of water

Chop the figs very fine, or put them through food grinder with the coarse blade. Put into canner kettle with 4 quarts of water and let stand overnight. The following day, bring to a boil for 30 minutes. While this liquid is still hot, stir in the sugar, then set aside to cool. Meanwhile, chop the apples as fine as coleslaw. When the fig liquid has cooled to lukewarm, add apples and chopped raisins. Set in a warm place to ferment for six weeks. Stir twice a week.

At the end of six weeks, strain through jelly bag, squeezing as dry as possible. Return to canner kettle for one more week of fermentation. Then strain through several thicknesses of cheesecloth, and allow to settle for two days longer. This last straining will remove any fine fig seeds which may have escaped the jelly bag. At the end of this settling period, siphon into clean sterilized bottles and cork lightly. When fermentation has stopped in the bottle, cork tightly and seal with paraffin. Keep for at least three months. This wine matures early, but, like all wines, aging does improve it.

APPLE-AND-CITRUS-FRUIT WINE

10 medium-sized McIntosh apples
3 grapefruit cut in ½" slices
3 lemons cut in ¼" slices
3 oranges cut in ¼" slices
8 cups of cane sugar
4 quarts of water
1 slice of white toast
1 ounce of wet yeast

Chop apples fine and put into canner kettle. Do not peel the oranges, lemons or grapefruit, but slice them with the peelings on. Add to chopped apples. Dissolve the sugar in 2 quarts of water over a low flame. Add the 2 remaining quarts of cool water, and then stir in the warm sugar-water. Moisten yeast with a few drops of water and spread on one side of the toast. Float toast, yeast side down, on the surface of the liquid. Set in a warm place to ferment for two weeks. Do not stir during this time.

At the end of this period, strain through jelly bag, but do *not* squeeze the fruit, for the bitterness of the grapefruit peel will go into the wine. In this instance it is wise to let the wine drip-dry. Return liquid to canner kettle for one more week's fermentation.

Then strain through several thicknesses of cheesecloth and return to canner kettle to settle for one day. Siphon into clean sterilized bottles and cork lightly. When fermentation is over, cork tightly and seal with paraffin. Keep for at least three months before opening.

RED RASPBERRY-CRAB APPLE WINE

1st two weeks:
8 pounds of crab apples
3 quarts of red raspberries, *or* 3 #2 cans of red raspberries
4 quarts of water
2nd two weeks:
6 cups of cane sugar
2 cups of white raisins
1 slice of white toast
1 ounce of wet yeast

88

Stem and quarter crab apples and chop very fine. Crush raspberries with a potato masher and put into canner kettle. Pour over them 2 quarts of boiling water. Set aside to cool to lukewarm. Then add the 2 remaining quarts of cool water and the chopped crab apples. Set in a warm place to ferment for two weeks. Stir every day, inverting the mash completely each time.

At the end of the two-week period, strain through jelly bag, squeezing quite dry. Return liquid to canner kettle, add chopped raisins and sugar. Stir well so that all of the sugar is dissolved. Moisten the yeast with a few drops of water, and spread on one side of the toast. Float the toast, yeast side down, on surface of liquid. Set in a warm place for two weeks more of fermentation. Then strain through several thicknesses of cheesecloth. Return to canner kettle to settle for two days more. Then siphon off into clean sterilized bottles, and cork lightly. When fermentation has stopped, cork tightly and seal with paraffin. Keep for at least six months.

CRAB-APPLE-AND-THORNAPPLE WINE

1st two weeks:
4 quarts of crab apples
4 quarts of ripe thornapples
2 cups of muscat raisins, finely chopped
4 quarts of water, room temperature
2nd two weeks:
6 cups of cane sugar
1 package of dry granulated yeast

Chop crab apples and thornapples to the consistency of coleslaw. Put chopped apples into canner kettle along with the finely chopped raisins. Add room-temperature water and stir very well. Set in a warm place to ferment for two weeks. Stir every day, inverting the fruit which rises to the surface.

At the end of this two-week period, strain through jelly bag, squeezing as dry as possible. Reserve 2 cups of the liquid for dissolving the sugar. Return the rest to canner kettle. Dissolve the sugar in the 2 cups of the liquid over a low flame, and bring to a rolling boil. While still hot, add to apple liquid in canner kettle. Sprinkle the dry granulated yeast over the surface and put in a warm place to ferment for two weeks longer. No stirring is necessary during this period.

Then strain through several thicknesses of cheesecloth and return to the canner kettle to settle for one day more. Siphon into clean sterilized bottles and cork lightly until fermentation is over. When there are no visible signs of fermentation, cork tightly and seal with paraffin. Keep this wine for six months. Avoid opening during the blossoming of either the crab apple or thornapple trees, as it goes through a slight fermentation then and will be turbid.

PEACH WINE

- 4 quarts of unpeeled quartered peaches (approximately 6 pounds)
- 3 cups of white raisins, finely chopped
- 8 cups of cane sugar
- 4 quarts of water
- 2 large shredded wheat biscuits, *or* 1½ cups of Wheat Chex

Put the quartered, unpeeled peaches into canner kettle. If fruit is on the very ripe side, mash gently with potato masher. If the fruit is not ripe enough to mash at this time, it can be done later during fermentation. Add the finely chopped raisins. Dissolve the sugar in 2 quarts of water over a low flame. Add remaining 2 quarts of cool water, and then follow with the hot sugar-water. Stir all very well. Break and crumble the shredded wheat and sprinkle over the surface. If you are using Wheat Chex, use whole. Set in a warm place to ferment for three weeks. Stir every day, mashing the fruit against the sides of the canner kettle.

At the end of this three-week period, strain through jelly bag, squeezing the pulp very dry. Return to canner kettle for one more week of fermentation. Then siphon into clean sterilized bottles and cork lightly.

This wine does a great deal of fermenting in the bottle, so test each bottle for signs of fermentation before final corking and sealing. Keep for three months from date of final corking. This wine matures early, but aging does give it a finer body and color.

PEACH-AND-PINEAPPLE WINE

- 4 quarts of unpeeled, quartered and stoned peaches (approximately 5 pounds) *or* 4 pounds of dried peaches

2 fresh pineapples, ripened in the sun for several days, *or*
    2 #2 cans of crushed pineapple
6 cups of cane sugar
4 quarts of water
1 shredded wheat biscuit, *or* 1 cup of Wheat Chex
1 package of dry granulated yeast

If the peaches are on the very ripe side, mash in the bottom of canner kettle with potato masher. If not, they can be mashed later in the fermentation process. Do not peel the fresh pineapple, but cut in pieces convenient for chopping and chop to about the fineness of the crushed pineapple available in cans. If using canned pineapple, add the fruit, juice and all, just as it comes from the can. Dissolve sugar in 2 quarts of water over a low flame. Add remaining 2 quarts of cool water, then follow with the hot sugar-water. Sprinkle in the crumbled shredded wheat; or, if using Wheat Chex, use whole. Sprinkle the dry granulated yeast over the surface, and put in a warm place to ferment for two weeks. Stir every day, mashing and crushing the fruit as much as possible.

At the end of two-week period, strain through jelly bag, squeezing pulp as dry as possible. Return liquid to canner kettle. Set in a warm place to ferment for two weeks longer without disturbing.

Then strain through several thicknesses of cheesecloth, and return to the canner kettle to settle for two days more. Siphon into clean sterilized bottles and cork lightly. When fermentation has ceased, cork tightly and seal with paraffin. Keep for six months.

PEACH-AND-APRICOT WINE
(From dried fruit)

1st day:
4 pounds of dried peach halves
4 pounds of dried apricots
4 quarts of water
2nd day:
2 cups of white raisins, finely chopped
8 cups of cane sugar
2 large shredded wheat biscuits, *or* 2 cups of Wheat Chex
1 package of dry granulated yeast

Soak apricots and peaches in the 4 quarts of water overnight. The following day, bring them to a boil for 45 minutes, or until tender enough to break with a fork. Set aside to cool to lukewarm. Then mash fruit in the water with potato masher. The fruit need not be chopped too fine, just broken up a bit. Add raisins, and stir in the sugar, making sure all is dissolved. Break up and crumble the shredded wheat into the liquid; if you are using Wheat Chex, add as they come from the box. Stir well, and sprinkle the dry granulated yeast over the surface. Put in a warm place to ferment for three weeks. Stir every day during this period.

At the end of three weeks, strain through jelly bag, squeezing very dry. Return to canner kettle to settle for two days more. Siphon into clean sterilized bottles and cork lightly until fermentation has ceased; then cork tightly and seal with paraffin. Keep this wine for three months. Like other peach wines, this matures early; however, aging for a longer time will give it deeper color and better flavor.

PEACH-AND-ORANGE WINE

- 4 quarts of quartered and unpeeled peaches (approximately 5 lbs.)
- 8 clear-skinned oranges (peelings to soak overnight)
- 8 cups of cane sugar
- 1 cup of white raisins, finely chopped
- 4 quarts of water
- 1 slice of white toast
- 1 ounce of wet yeast

Peel oranges as thin as possible with a potato peeler. Put peelings into separate mixing bowl. Bring 1 quart of water to a rapid boil and pour over orange peelings; set aside overnight.

Meanwhile, chop peaches quite fine and put into canner kettle. Squeeze the juice from peeled oranges and strain into peaches. Dissolve the sugar in 1 quart of water over a low flame. Add the remaining 2 quarts of cool water to the fruit, and follow with the hot sugar-water. Stir all very well to distribute the sugar. Set this aside overnight, too.

The following day, strain the water from orange peelings into mixture in the canner kettle. Discard orange peelings; do *not* add them to the wine. Moisten the yeast with a few drops of water and spread on one side of the toast. Float the toast, yeast side down, on the surface of liquid. Set in a warm place to ferment for two weeks. Stir every day, crushing fruit against sides of canner kettle.

At the end of this two-week period, strain through jelly bag, squeezing very dry. Return liquid to canner kettle for two more weeks of undisturbed fermentation. Then strain through several thicknesses of cheesecloth and return again to the canner kettle to settle for two days more.

Siphon off into clean sterilized bottles and cork lightly until fermentation has ceased. When there are no more signs of activity in the bottles, cork tightly and seal with paraffin. Keep for six months.

HEAVY SPICED APRICOT WINE

6 cups of dried apricots (soak overnight)
5 cups of cane sugar
3 cups of light brown cane sugar
2 cups of muscat raisins, finely chopped
1/4 lb. of candied ginger, finely chopped
1 lemon cut in 1/4" slices
1 orange cut in 1/4" slices
4 quarts of water
1 slice of whole wheat toast
1 ounce of wet yeast

Soak apricots overnight in 2 quarts of water. Next morning, bring to a slow boil in the same water. Stir frequently to prevent its sticking to the bottom of the pan. Replace any water lost in boiling. Remove from flame and add the white and brown sugar, stirring well so that it is all dissolved. Put into canner kettle and add chopped raisins and ginger; then add the sliced lemon and orange and the remaining 2 quarts of water. Moisten yeast with a few drops of water and spread on one side of the toast. Float toast, yeast side down, on surface of liquid. Set in a warm place to ferment for four weeks. Stir at least three times a week.

At the end of four-week period, strain through jelly bag, squeezing the pulp very dry. Return to canner kettle to settle for three days longer. Siphon into clean sterilized bottles and cork lightly. When you are sure fermentation has ceased, cork tightly and seal with paraffin. Keep for at least four months, though eight makes it a much better wine. At the end of a year's aging, this wine has the flavor and consistency of good apricot liqueur.

PLAIN PEAR WINE

4 quarts of chopped unpeeled ripe pears (approximately 5 lbs.)
3 cups of white raisins, finely chopped
6 cups of cane sugar
1 cup of light brown sugar
4 quarts of water
1 shredded wheat biscuit, *or* 1 cup of Wheat Chex
    grape brandy (optional)

The pears should be ripe enough so you can pull the stems out without any effort. If pears are not very ripe, set them in the sun for a day or two. Quarter each pear, and with the tip of a teaspoon remove seeds from each section. Pear seeds are bitter and can be detected in the wine. Chop as fine as coleslaw.

Put the finely chopped pears, finely chopped raisins, and the crumbled shredded wheat into canner kettle. When using Wheat Chex, add whole. Dissolve brown and white sugar in 2 quarts of water over a low flame. Bring to a boil, then set aside to cool to lukewarm.

Add the 2 remaining quarts of cold water to the mixture, then add the lukewarm sugar-water. Stir the entire mash very well to distribute the sugar. Set in a warm place for three weeks. Stir every day, breaking up the fruit against the sides of the canner kettle.

At the end of this three-week period, strain through jelly bag, squeezing very dry. Return liquid to canner kettle. Set in a warm place to ferment for two weeks longer. No stirring is necessary during this last fermentation.

At the end of this period (this makes five weeks in all), strain liquid through several thicknesses of cheesecloth. It should be ladled or siphoned into cheesecloth, as great care must be taken to prevent any of the "cloud" which forms at the bottom from getting in the wine. This cloudy wine should be put into a two-quart jar to continue settling for a day or so; then it can be bottled. The clear wine should be returned to the canner kettle to settle for two days. This settling period may seem unnecessary, but experience has taught me that a much clearer wine results. After the settling, siphon into clean sterilized bottles and cork lightly. Again, take care to keep the siphon off the bottom of the canner kettle. When fermentation has ceased in the bottle, cork tightly and seal with paraffin.

Pears are a rather bland fruit and make a bland wine. If you desire more character in your wine, add 1/4 pound of candied ginger, finely chopped, at the same time as the raisins. If you desire heat along with the spicy taste, also add ten or twelve black peppercorns.

There was an attempt to market pear wine commercially in this country at one time. However, due to its blandness, winemakers found it had to be fortified up to 20% with pear brandy. Homemade wine can be fortified, too, for better results. I find that using a good grade of grape brandy gives a wonderful flavor. I add this just before the two-day settling period, using about 2 cups of brandy to the gallon.

In France and Germany there is a pear champagne which is made in much the same manner; however, it is bottled and corked tightly while in the fermenting stage, giving it effervescence when opened.

PEAR-AND-PINEAPPLE WINE

4 quarts of chopped ripe pears (approximately 5 lbs.)
2 fresh pineapples, ripened in the sun, *or* 2 #2 cans of crushed pineapple
8 cups of cane sugar
4 quarts of water
1 piece of white toast
1 ounce of wet yeast

Be sure pears are ripe enough to pull out stems. Remove stems, but do not peel. Cut in quarters and remove seed sections with tip of a teaspoon. Chop as fine as you would chop coleslaw.

Remove the stem and bottom of the pineapple, but do not peel. Cut into slices, and chop as fine as crushed pineapple. If using canned pineapple, add as it comes from the can, juice and all. Combine chopped pears and pineapple in canner kettle. Dissolve sugar in 1 quart of water over a low flame. Add the 3 quarts of cool water first, and follow with the hot sugar-water. Stir well to distribute the sugar. Moisten the yeast with a few drops of water, and spread on toast. Float toast, yeast side down, on surface of the liquid. Set in a warm place to ferment for two weeks. Stir gently from the bottom every day.

At end of two-week period, strain through jelly bag, squeezing pulp very dry. Return liquid to canner kettle for two more weeks of undisturbed fermentation.

Then strain through several thicknesses of cheesecloth by siphoning. The cloudy wine at the bottom should be put in a separate two-quart jar to settle. Return the clear wine to canner kettle to settle for two days longer. Then siphon into clean sterilized bottles, being sure to keep the siphon off bottom of kettle. Cork lightly, and when fermentation has ceased, cork tightly and seal with paraffin. Keep for six months. The cloudy wine set aside in the fruit jar can be siphoned off into a bottle and corked in the same manner. If it fails to clear in a reasonable amount of time, add 2 crushed eggshells; these will draw the solids to the bottom, giving a clear, slightly paler wine.

PLAIN PLUM WINE

1st day:
4 quarts of halved and pitted ripe plums
4 quarts of boiling water
8 cups of cane sugar
2nd day:
2 cups of muscat raisins, finely chopped
2 cups of cracked wheat
1 package of dry granulated yeast

Chop plum halves to the consistency of coleslaw; set aside in large mixing bowl. Put 4 quarts of water into canner kettle with the sugar. Place over a low flame and stir until sugar is dissolved. Bring to a rapid boil for 5 minutes. Remove liquid from fire and, while still boiling hot, add chopped plums. This will set the red color contained in the plum skins. Set aside overnight.

The following day, stir in the raisins and cracked wheat. Sprinkle the dry granulated yeast over the surface. Set in a warm place to ferment for two weeks. Stir and invert the mash every day.

At the end of two-week period, strain through jelly bag, squeezing quite dry. Return liquid to canner kettle to settle for two days longer. Siphon into clean sterilized bottles and cork lightly until fermentation has ceased. After fermentation is over, cork tightly and seal with paraffin. Keep for six months.

Plum wine goes through a mild fermentation when the plum blossoms are on the trees, so avoid opening wine at this time.

HEAVY PLUM WINE

4 quarts of pitted and halved Italian plums
2 quarts of chopped red beets (approximately 3 lbs.)
8 cups of cane sugar
4 quarts of water
1 package of dry granulated yeast

Scrub beets well, removing stem and tail ends. Do not peel. Cut into quarters, and chop very fine. Put chopped beets into a pan with 3 quarts of water and boil for 30 minutes.

While the beets are boiling, chop plums to the consistency of coleslaw. Put the plums into canner kettle and pour boiling-hot beets and water over them. Stir well, and put in a warm place to ferment for two weeks. Stir every day, inverting the mash completely.

At the end of this two-week period, strain through jelly bag and squeeze very dry. Return liquid to canner kettle. Dissolve sugar in remaining 1 quart of water over a low flame. While still hot, stir into the plum-and-beet liquid. When lukewarm, sprinkle dry yeast over the surface and put in a warm place to ferment for two weeks more.

Then strain through several thicknesses of cheesecloth and return to canner kettle to settle for two days more. Siphon into clean sterilized bottles and cork lightly until fermentation has ceased. Then cork tightly and seal with paraffin. Keep for six months.

PINEAPPLE WINE
(Made from fresh pineapple)

1st day:
4 large fresh pineapples
2 quarts of water
2 cups of white raisins, finely chopped
2nd day:
2 quarts of water
8 cups of cane sugar
1 package of dry granulated yeast

Ripen pineapples out of doors on sunny side of the house

for several days before making wine. They should be ripe enough so you can pull center spurs from the stalk with very little effort. Remove the stalks and the bottom core bud, but do not peel. The peelings contain many active wine yeast cells.

Cut pineapples into slices convenient for chopping; then chop, core and all, very fine. Put into canner kettle with chopped raisins. Add 2 quarts of water and set aside overnight.

The following day, dissolve the sugar in remaining 2 quarts of water over low flame. While still hot, stir into pineapple mixture. When lukewarm, sprinkle dry granulated yeast over the surface. Put in a warm place to ferment for two weeks. Stir every day, inverting and mashing the fruit.

At the end of this two-week period, strain through jelly bag, squeezing very dry. Return the liquid to canner kettle for one more week's fermentation. Do not disturb during this time.

Then siphon off into clean sterilized bottles and cork lightly until fermentation has ceased. When there are no longer signs of fermentation, cork tightly and seal with paraffin. Keep for six months.

CANTALOUPE WINE

5 large cantaloupes, very ripe
1 cup of white raisins, finely chopped
4 clear-skinned lemons, cut into 1/4" slices
6 cups of cane sugar
4 quarts of room-temperature water
1 package of dry granulated yeast

The homegrown variety of melon is best for this wine. By homegrown I mean those luscious ripe melons that the local farmers bring to market. Cantaloupes shipped in partially green, and not fully sun ripened, will not give wine the same rich flavor.

Peel the cantaloupes with an ordinary potato peeler. Go over them several times to get all of the white section under the peeling. Cut cantaloupe in half while holding it over the canner kettle; in this way you will capture all the juice around the seeds. Then cut up smaller and mash the meat, seeds and all, with the potato masher. Add sliced lemons and chopped raisins. Add 3 quarts of water. Dissolve the sugar in remaining 1 quart of water over a low flame. While still hot, stir into cantaloupe mixture. When lukewarm, sprinkle the dry granulated yeast over the surface. Put in a warm place to ferment for one week. Stir this mash very well during this time, mashing against the sides of the kettle to break up melon pieces further.

At the end of this week, strain through jelly bag, squeezing well to extract all of the juice. Return the liquid to the canner kettle and put in a warm place to ferment for an additional week.

At the end of this period (this makes two weeks in all), strain through several thicknesses of cheesecloth. Return to canner kettle to settle for two days more. Siphon into clean sterilized bottles and cork lightly. This wine may have to spend three weeks in the lightly corked stage of fermentation, for it is quite active. Watch it carefully, and when tapping each bottle brings no signs of fermentation, you are ready to fasten corks tightly and seal with paraffin. Keep for at least six months.

CHAPTER VIII

Behold the Grape

The science of grape culture for winemaking is one of the most complex in the world. There have been countless tomes written on the grape and its conversion into wine—and still more tomes written on the comparison of the qualities of these various wines.

The Concord grape is America's own baby, and, sad to relate, has been scorned when compared with other grapes. But year after year the growers of this beautiful fruit are improving their stock, and I think the time will come when the Concord grape will come into its own as a universally recognized winemaker.

However, my confidence in and fondness for this grape seems to be shared with a few friends only. Almost every book on vine culture for wine takes at least two nasty punches at my beloved Concord grape. I'll concede a lot of the critical points they make, but until there are other varieties of grapes on the supermarket counters in equal abundance, and at a really reasonable price, give me the Concord!

Concord grapes, handled correctly, make a wine beautiful in color and excellent in flavor. One of the most frequent criticisms is that the Concord is low in natural sugars. Granted, but something can be done about this. The following recipes will show how to remedy this lack of natural sugar successfully.

The first rule for successful grape wine is: Do *not* wash the grapes! Cleanliness is a virtue, but washing grapes destroys the very thing which will make fine wine—the natural yeast cells. Most market grapes come from vineyards in open country. Since they are picked in clusters, human contact with the actual fruit is practically nil.

It has been found that wine yeast cells exist in the soil of the vineyard at all times. Right after the vines have bloomed and grapes have formed, the yeast in the soil is so high that a drop of it added to the proper warm nutritive solution will act exactly as does the yeast bought at a grocery.

100

Wasps are given the credit for carrying yeast cells to the grapes. If you find grapes in the basket that are split open from being overripe, do not destroy them, for they teem with active yeast cells left there by wasps. These insects have a liking for grape juice, but being small, weak creatures, they have to depend on nature to open the grapes for them. While they are having their sips of nectar, they probably leave several healthy colonies of wine yeast cells behind with their footprints. Without these cells there could be no wine.

Getting back to the subject of cleaning grapes—naturally, if you find grapes that have green mold on them, you should throw them away. If the grapes are actually dusty and gritty, and you feel they must be washed, the best method is to rinse them quickly, in clusters, under cold running water.

The stems of grapes are another object of contention among winemakers. Some part of winemaking practice has trickled in from Europe; there, in most cases, the stems and all are thrown into the vats. Stems on most European grapes are of a finer texture and a sweeter flavor than those of the Concord grape. I have found that the stem of the Concord gives a bitter, acrid taste to wine; too, the stems of these grapes are quite woody and thick. When making wine from Concord grapes, it is better to forget the stems completely. I have made Concord grape wine both with and without the stems and greatly prefer that made from the grapes alone. Stripping the grapes off is a little extra work, but it does make a better wine.

Most books on winemaking from grapes are rather vague about measurements. All housewives have made things in a hurry without measuring too carefully, only to have flat failures staring them in the face. I still maintain that the cooks of the old school who say "as much water as an eggshell will hold, or as much flour as you can hold in your hand" have more failures because of measurements than up-to-date cooks who use level standard measurements. Many old wine books give measurements which are as inaccurate as the eggshell system. I have one recipe in my collection which calls for a dishpan full of grapes. Well, dishpans do vary in size.

All grapes are sold by the pound—that is, not an actual pound of little round grapes, but a pound of stems and grapes combined to make the weight. Some seasons, grapes are very small, due to lack of moisture; then again, there are season in which grapes are real whoppers. When they are packed at the vineyard, there is an exact weight standard. If the weather is dry and hot while the grapes are being shipped, a pound of this weight will disappear into thin air. To avoid customer difficulties, most Concord vineyards pack a little over the weight standard set.

The first method of buying grapes I shall deal with is the small basket. This measures about a foot long by about six inches across. The stamped weight on this basket is five pounds. The actual grapes, minus stems, weigh about three. One of these baskets will usually yield about three quart measures, loosely packed, of grapes stripped from the stems.

The next method of buying grapes is in the large basket. This usually runs between 16 and 18 pounds. Again, the weight at the vineyard will be clearly stamped on the cover or side of the basket. The yield of one of these large baskets in stripped grapes is about ten quart measures.

If you have a kitchen scale, put a dishpan on it and adjust the scale to zero. Then put the cleaned grapes into the dishpan to get the exact weight. This will give you a rule to follow for a sweet grape wine: You will need exactly half the weight of the grapes in sugar. In other words, if you have five pounds of grapes you will need two and a half pounds of sugar. If you have no scale, estimate by dry measure. One quart of grapes will require one pint of sugar.

This makes a sweet wine. If you prefer a dry wine, diminish the sugar by half. Before bottling the wine, taste it; if it is not sweet enough, add more sugar.

The sugar ratio in the previous paragraphs was included for those people who are fortunate enough to have Concords growing nearby. Many vineyards will let you pick your own, charging by the bushel. Since there is no easy way of telling how many large or small baskets make a bushel, the kitchen scale will serve as a guide. This sugar ratio can be used for other varieties of homegrown grapes, too.

The recipes which follow have been tried and tested, so there will be no need for you to go through the measuring process if you buy grapes by the basket.

HEAVY GRAPE WINE

2 small baskets of Concord grapes (approximately 5 lbs. each)
6 cups of cane sugar

102

Strip grapes from stems directly into canner kettle. Remove any that have signs of green mold. If some grapes are broken open, do not throw them away, for they contain very active winemaking yeast cells. Crush grapes with a potato masher until all the skins are broken, and until juice that rises around the masher is deep red in color. Add sugar, one cup at a time, and stir after each addition until it is completely dissolved. Put mixture in a warm place to ferment for six weeks. Stir every day, mashing grapes against sides of canner kettle. Also invert the mash completely in this daily stirring operation.

At the end of this six-week period, strain through jelly bag, twisting until the pulp is very dry. Return to canner kettle and let stand for two weeks more of fermentation. Do not disturb during this period, as the wine also settles for bottling at this time.

After two weeks, siphon off into clean sterilized bottles. Keep siphoning hose well off bottom of kettle. Fit the corks in the necks of the bottles very loosely until fermentation has ceased. Then fasten the corks tightly and seal with paraffin. Keep for at least three months, though at the end of six months the wine is better.

LIGHT GRAPE WINE

2 small baskets of Concord grapes (weight approximately 5 lbs. each)
3 quarts of cold water
10 cups of cane sugar (add after one week)

Strip grapes from stems into canner kettle. Do not crush, but add 3 quarts of water to the whole grapes. Put in a warm place to ferment for 1 week without disturbing.

Then stir and mash the grapes, breaking up as many as possible. Stir in the sugar a cup at a time, making sure after each addition that all of it is dissolved. Set in a warm place to ferment for six weeks more. Stir every day during this period; with every stirring, invert the mash and break it up against the sides of the canner kettle.

At the end of this six weeks' fermentation, strain through jelly bag, squeezing very dry. Return to canner kettle for another week of fermentation and settling. Then siphon into clean sterilized bottles and cork lightly. When fermentation has definitely ceased, cork tightly and seal with paraffin. Keep for six months.

CONCORD GRAPE-RASPBERRY WINE

1st two weeks:
1 small basket of Concord grapes (weight approximately 5 lbs.)
4 quarts of tepid water
2nd two weeks:
8 cups of cane sugar
3 quarts of black raspberries, *or* 2 #2 cans of black raspberries

Strip grapes from stems into canner kettle. Crush with potato masher until all are broken and juice which rises around the masher is bright red. Add 4 quarts of water and stir well. Set in a warm place to ferment for two weeks. Stir every day, inverting the mash completely each time.

At the end of two-week period, strain through jelly bag, squeezing as dry as possible. In a separate kettle, mash raspberries with potato masher until all are broken. Add 2 cups of the grape liquid to the raspberries; then put them over a low flame to simmer for 20 minutes. Stir frequently so berries do not scorch. If using canned raspberries, no boiling is necessary, but add them just as they come from the can, juice and all. Stir the sugar in the grape juice, making sure all is dissolved; add the hot raspberries and set in a warm place to ferment for two weeks more.

Then strain through several thicknesses of cheesecloth. Siphon immediately into clean sterilized bottles and cork lightly. When fermentation has ceased, cork tightly and seal with paraffin. Keep for one year; a very fine wine will reward your patience.

DARK RED GRAPE WINE

In many respects, grapes grown in the United States are different from those grown in the wine regions of Europe. The Continental grapes have skins that tightly adhere to the meat, while the meat of most of our American varieties can be pinched out with two fingers. Here is a wonderful recipe which takes advantage of the loose covering of our grapes to make an incomparable wine.

2 small baskets of Concord grapes
10 cups of cane sugar
4 quarts of water (3 quarts to be added later)

Have ready a large (five-quart) mixing bowl in addition to canner kettle. Strip grapes from stems one by one, and pinch meat out of each grape. Put the meaty portion into canner kettle and the grape skins into mixing bowl. Dissolve the sugar in one quart of the water over a low flame. Add the hot sugar-water to the grape centers in the canner kettle; stir well, and set aside to ferment for one week.

Chop grape skins as fine as possible. Working on only one cup at a time will make the task easier. Return to mixing bowl and cover with remaining 3 quarts of water. Set aside in a warm place to ferment separately for one week.

At the end of this time, strain juce from grape-skin mixture through jelly bag, squeezing very dry. Add to grape-meat mixture in canner kettle and set in a warm place to ferment for one week more. Then strain the whole mixture through jelly bag, squeezing well to extract all the juice. Return to canner kettle to settle for one week more. (This is a total of three weeks' fermentation.) Siphon into clean sterilized bottles and cork lightly. Before fastening the corks tightly, tap each bottle for fermentation bubbles up the sides. When bubbles have completely stopped, fasten the corks, and seal with paraffin. Keep this wine for at least six months.

GRAPE WINE WITH GRAPE LEAVES

Many of us can remember our mother's or grandmother's preserved pickles with a grape leaf in each jar. This leaf gave a sharp delicate flavor to the pickles. So it is with the following recipe; an indescribably fine flavor is imparted to the wine by the addition of grape leaves. If you know of someone who has a grape vine, bearing or not, ask for ten leaves. Pick perfect leaves with no brown spots.

1 small basket of Concord grapes (approximately 5 lbs.)
10 grape leaves
4 quarts room-temperature water
8 cups of cane sugar
1 package of dry granulated yeast

Strip grapes from stems into canner kettle. Mash well with a potato masher. Add the whole grape leaves and 3 quarts of water. Dissolve sugar in remaining quart of water over a low flame. While still hot, stir into grape mixture. Sprinkle the dry yeast over the surface and set in a warm place to ferment for one week.

At the end of this time, strain through jelly bag, squeezing very dry. Return liquid to canner kettle to ferment undisturbed for two weeks more.

Strain through several thicknesses of cheesecloth and siphon immediately into clean sterilized bottles. Cork lightly until fermentation has ceased, and then cork tightly and seal with paraffin. Keep at least three months; six months of aging will give you a much finer wine.

CONCORD GRAPE-GOOSEBERRY WINE

1 small basket of Concord grapes
2 quarts of gooseberries—a little underripe
10 grape leaves (optional)
4 quarts of cold water
8 cups of cane sugar
2 cups of muscat raisins, finely chopped
1 package of dry granulated yeast

Strip grapes from stems into canner kettle. Head and tail the gooseberries, and add to grapes. Mash both grapes and gooseberries well with a potato masher. Juice which gathers around the masher must be bright red. Add grape leaves, finely chopped raisins, 3 quarts of water. Dissolve sugar in remaining quart of water over a low flame. While still hot, add to grape-gooseberry mixture. Sprinkle the dry granulated yeast over the surface. Set in a warm place to ferment for two weeks.

After this time, strain through jelly bag, squeezing the pulp as dry as possible. Return to canner kettle for one more week of fermentation and settling. Then siphon into clean sterilized bottles, corking lightly until fermentation has ceased. When fermentation is over, cork tightly and seal with paraffin. Keep for six months.

This is a very refreshing, sharp, dry wine; it goes well with rich fowl such as duck and goose.

Along most rural highways and byways grow two elusive vines which are in great demand and which mature at the same time—wild grapes and bittersweet.* Both of these beautiful plants are ravaged each year by careless people—yanked from their moorings by the handful. Once the wild grape or bittersweet is uprooted, it is finished. Both should be cut with scissors or a sharp knife, and with the same care that flowers are picked in a garden. Most states regulate the picking of bittersweet, but the wild grape is unprotected by the law.

Wild grapes, naturally, have a wild taste. Wine made from the wild grape alone is apt to be very dry—or, as people who like a sweet taste describe it, "sourish." Personally, I like the dryness and the taste of wild grape wine. If you find a roadside patch of wild grapes, pick them carefully, either stripping the individual grapes from the stems or cutting the stem close to the fruit with a knife or scissors. Be careful of getting the juice on your clothes, for there is nothing on earth which seems to remove the stain. It is so potent a coloring agent that Indians used to use it as a textile dye.

The common wild grape of the United States grows and looks like a miniature Concord. If you have any doubt as to what you are picking, send a specimen to your State Agricultural Department. Remember, there are several varieties of deadly poisonous berries which grow in clusters just as grapes do.

DRY WILD GRAPE WINE

4 quarts of wild grapes
8 cups of cane sugar
3 quarts of tepid water

For some reason or other the stems of wild grapes do not impart the bitterness that Concord grape stems do. Do not leave any of the very heavy stems on, though the smaller ones suspending the grapes can be put right into the wine mash.

Put the wild grapes into canner kettle and mash well with

---

* Not to be confused with *Solanum Dulcamara* or deadly nightshade.

a potato masher. Dissolve the sugar in 1 quart of water over a low flame.

Add the remaining 2 quarts of water to the crushed grapes and pour in the sugar-water while it is still hot. Mix very well, so that all of the sugar is evenly distributed. Put in a warm place to ferment for four weeks. Stir every day, turning over the mash completely so that the grapes which have risen to the top are pushed back to the bottom.

At the end of this four-week period, strain through jelly bag, squeezing as dry as possible. Return to canner kettle to settle for one week longer.

Then siphon off into clean sterilized bottles and cork lightly. Watch closely for the stoppage of fermentation; the moment you are sure it is over, cork tightly and seal with paraffin. Keep for six months. This wine, like domestic grape wine, goes through a fermentation period in the spring and fall, so avoid opening the bottles in either of these two periods. It will be turbid and cloudy if you do.

WILD-GRAPE-AND-CONCORD-GRAPE WINE

1 quart of wild grapes
1 small basket of Concord grapes (approximately 5 lbs. in weight)
6 cups of cane sugar
4 quarts of water

This is a wonderful wine to make if you have been able to find only a few wild grapes.

Strip Concord grapes from stems directly into canner kettle. Add the wild grapes without removing them from their stems. Mash together with a potato masher until juice around the masher is bright red.

Dissolve the sugar in 1 quart of water over a very low flame. Add the 3 remaining quarts to the wild-grape-and-Concord-grape mixture. While the sugar-water is still hot, stir it in, too. Stir the entire mash very well, so that the sugar is thoroughly mixed throughout the mash. Set in a warm place to ferment for four weeks. Stir every day, being sure that the grapes which have risen to the top are pushed to the bottom.

At the end of four weeks, strain through jelly bag, squeezing as dry as possible. Return this juice to canner kettle for two more weeks of fermentation.

After this period (this is six weeks in all) siphon off into clean sterilized bottles and cork lightly. Watch the wine carefully, and when you are sure the fermentation has ceased, cork tightly and seal with paraffin. Keep for at least six months. A year's wait is very rewarding.

There Are Other Grapes, Too

There are many grapes on the market besides the Concord. Branching out will cost a little more money, but the wine is well worth the investment.

At one of our large markets, I found the manager more than willing to part with all the grapes which fall from those picturelike clusters displayed on the counter. As his clerks unpack the boxes of grapes, he sets aside a separate box for all that fall off, and for the bunches which are not in perfect condition. He sells the whole lot to me for about a dollar. At this one particular market, they have found that almost one box out of seven is unsalable. This may seem an appalling waste to the housewife; but to the winemaker it's a golden opportunity. When buying grapes for showpiece fruit bowls or for table eating, naturally you want choice clusters. However, when you are going to mash them to smithereens for wine, you care very little for their visual beauty.

At times I've got small green seedless grapes in this manner, or perhaps all Tokay. Then again, I've got boxes that were a mixture of several kinds. They all make wonderful wine.

A very good time to look for bargains in grapes for winemaking is just before a long week end when the stores are going to be closed. Most dealers are glad to find a buyer for perishable fruits, and will dispose of them at a bargain. Getting acquainted with the manager of the local large market can pay real dividends in fine grapes for wine. Leave your telephone number with him, and remind him from time to time that you are interested in bargain grapes. Chances are he'll be only too pleased to have you take them off his hands.

SWEET GREEN GRAPE WINE

5 lbs. of seedless green grapes
4 quarts of tepid water
6 cups of cane sugar
1 package of dry granulated yeast

Small seedless grapes need not be stripped from the stems. Put stems, grapes and all right into the canner kettle. Naturally, if there are any large rough stems, they should be cut away. Mash the grapes well with a potato masher. Add 3 quarts of tepid water. Dissolve sugar in remaining one quart of water over a low flame, and while it is still hot add to grape mixture. Stir very well to distribute the sugar. Sprinkle the dry granulated yeast over the surface and put in a warm place to ferment for two weeks. Stir every day, inverting the mash completely with each stirring.

At the end of two weeks, strain through jelly bag, squeezing the pulp very dry. Return liquid to canner kettle and set in a warm place to ferment for two weeks longer.

Then strain through several thicknesses of cheesecloth, and immediately siphon into clean sterilized bottles. Cork lightly until all fermentation has ceased, and then cork tightly and seal with paraffin. Keep for six months.

DRY GREEN GRAPE WINE

10 lbs. of seedless green grapes
4 quarts of water

Snip off large rough stems, but leave on all stems to which grapes are directly attached. Put into canner kettle, and mash just enough so they will be submerged by the 4 quarts of water. Put in a warm place to ferment for four weeks. During this time, stir and crush fruit every day. Be sure to invert the mash completely every time you stir it.

At the end of this fermentation period, strain through jelly bag, squeezing pulp very dry. Return liquid to canner kettle for another two weeks of fermentation.

Then strain through several thicknesses of cheesecloth. Siphon immediately into clean sterilized bottles and cork lightly. This wine will be active in the bottles a little longer than most, so tap each bottle for fermentation bubbles before fastening corks and sealing with paraffin. Keep for at least six months, though it will be better after a year.

LIGHT-GREEN-GRAPE-AND-FIG WINE

3 lbs. of seedless green grapes
3 lbs. of dried light figs

3 lbs. of tart apples
4 quarts of water
8 cups of cane sugar

Soak figs in 4 quarts of water overnight in canner kettle. The following day, put them on to boil for 45 minutes, or until they break apart when pierced with a fork. Remove liquid from stove, and stir in sugar, making sure all of it is dissolved. Set aside to cool to lukewarm.

While cooling, chop apples as fine as coleslaw; in a separate bowl, mash grapes well with a potato masher. When the liquid has grown lukewarm, add chopped apples and mashed grapes. Set in a warm place to ferment for four weeks. Stir every day during this period, being sure to invert mash with each stirring.

At the end of this time, strain through jelly bag, squeezing pulp very dry. Return liquid to canner kettle to settle and ferment for one more week. Then siphon into clean sterilized bottles and cork lightly until fermentation has ceased. When you are sure there are no more signs of fermentation, cork tightly and seal with paraffin. Keep for six months. This is a wonderful dessert wine.

TOKAY GRAPE WINE

Our California Tokay grapes are wonderful winemakers. There are times when they can be purchased very reasonably at the market. Tokays have a high sugar content, give a wonderful color to wine, and are a good mixer with other fruits.

5 lbs. of Tokay grapes
8 cups of cane sugar
4 quarts of water

Cut away largest stems. Put grapes and smaller stems into canner kettle. Mash well with potato masher. Dissolve sugar in 2 quarts of the water over a low flame. Add remaining 2 quarts of water, and follow with the hot sugar-water. Stir all very well so that the sugar is evenly distributed. Put in a warm place to ferment for three weeks. Stir every day during this period, and invert the mash each time.

After three weeks, strain through jelly bag, squeezing pulp very dry. Return liquid to canner kettle and allow to ferment and settle for one week longer. Then siphon into clean sterilized bottles and cork lightly. When fermentation has ceased, cork tightly and seal with paraffin. Keep this wine for at least six months.

If you can get a large amount of Tokay grapes, reduce the amount of water. This will give your wine a somewhat higher alcohol content.

TOKAY-PEAR WINE

Here is a blending of two flavors that go together like ham and eggs. This is one of my favorite wines.

    5 lbs. of Tokay grapes
    5 lbs. of overripe Bartlett pears
    8 cups of cane sugar
    4 quarts of tepid water

Cut away the bigger stems, and put grapes and the finer stems into canner kettle. Mash grapes well with potato masher. Pull stems from the Bartletts, and chop very fine with bladed chopping knife. Add chopped pears to grapes, then add 3 quarts of water. Dissolve sugar in the remaining quart of water, over low flame. While this sugar-water is still hot, stir it into grape mixture. Stir very well so that the sugar is evenly distributed. Set in a warm place to ferment for three weeks. Stir every day, and invert the mash completely every time you stir.

After three weeks, strain through jelly bag, squeezing pulp very dry. Return liquid to canner kettle to settle and ferment for one week longer. Then siphon off into clean sterilized bottles and cork lightly. This wine is active in the bottle, so tap each bottle for signs of bubbles on the sides before fastening the corks tightly and sealing with paraffin. Keep for six months; however, a year's aging is worth the time.

A Little More about Grapes

One of the most amazing things about the grape is that it follows the four seasons of the year very closely.

When winter puts the vineyard to rest, the wine will sleep, too. However, when spring arrives, and things in the earth start seeking growth, so does the wine begin to stir. When the sap goes up into the vines, grape wines may become cloudy. When the vines burst into bloom, the wine will go through a period of fermentation. While the grape is on the vine, growing and absorbing sunshine, and harboring wine yeast cells, the wine is content and peaceful. When the grape on the vine is ripe, the wine will go through another period of fermentation. If, in the fermentation periods of either spring or autumn, you happen to open a bottle of grape wine, you will detect a certain sharp quality that was not there in winter or midsummer.

To sum up, I am reminded of a minister who was explaining to his congregation a phenomenon of nature. He more or less ran out of words and was hedging in a nervous manner. All at once he blurted, "Well . . . all I can say is, 'Somebody's stirrin' this thing.'"

CHAPTER IX

Rhubarb's Not Only a Cat, But—

Rhubarb has been famous as everything from a sure cure for scurvy to a tough shaggy cat who owned a baseball team. Its fame is not surprising, for rhubarb is just plain wonderful stuff. It is very high in Vitamin C, and it is also the base for a lot of wonderful homemade wines!

Rhubarb is inexpensive to buy. However, if you have several plants of your own, you know only too well that if left to their own devices, they grow like green monsters. Rhubarb will grow almost anywhere in any soil. It is found in gardens from Maine to California. It is practically blight free, and is very hardy.

There is only one caution to bear in mind about rhubarb— *the leaves are highly poisonous.* Never, under any conditions, use the leaves for *anything* but garbage—and even then, be sure they are wrapped and tied securely.

Some city-bred friends of ours bought a little four-acre country place and, that first summer, found rhubarb growing like fury. This city-farmer housewife gathered it and made canned rubarb sauce. The leaves looked so pretty, and seemed to her so rich in chlorophyll, that she mixed them with the dinner for her husband's pride and joy—his two pet pigs. These poor pigs just laid down in their pen the next day and died.

The farmer called in a veterinarian, who in turn called in the County Agricultural Agent. The stomach contents of the pigs was analyzed—rhubarb leaves with their high count of calcium oxalate caused their death! I have always wondered why rhubarb was sold absolutely bare of its leaves in the city markets. Now I know.

Here are a few of the wines made from rhubarb. I know that there must be hundreds more. If you have any exotic recipes up your sleeve, I would appreciate hearing from you.

GOLDEN RHUBARB WINE

4 quarts of rhubarb, cut into ½" pieces
4 quarts of cold water
1 lemon cut in ¼" slices
1 orange cut in ¼" slices
3 cups of muscat raisins, finely chopped
8 cups of cane sugar
1 package of dry granulated yeast

Put the cut-up rhubarb into canner kettle. Add 4 quarts of cold water and set in a warm place to ferment for two weeks. Stir every day, breaking up the rhubarb either by hand or with a potato masher.

At the end of two weeks strain through jelly bag, squeezing pulp as dry as possible. Return liquid to canner kettle, with the exception of 3 cups. Dissolve sugar in the 3 cups of liquid over a low flame. While still hot, stir into original rhubarb liquid. Add chopped raisins, sliced lemon and orange. Sprinkle dry granulated yeast over the surface and put in a warm place to ferment for two weeks longer.

At the end of this period (this makes four weeks in all) strain through several thicknesses of cheesecloth. Return liquid to canner kettle to settle for two days longer. Siphon off into clean sterilized bottles and cork lightly. When fermentation has ceased, cork tightly and seal with paraffin.

Keep this wine for at least one year. It will develop a very fine body and flavor in that time. This is one of the wines to which the addition of an ounce of glycerin before the settling is a great improvement; it strengthens the body of the wine greatly.

RED RHUBARB WINE

1st two weeks:
4 quarts of rhubarb, cut into ½" pieces
3 lbs. of red beets, unpeeled
4 quarts of cold water
8 cups of cane sugar
2nd stage:
2 cups of muscat raisins, finely chopped
¼ lb. of candied ginger, finely chopped

12 black peppercorns
1 package of dry granulated yeast

Scrub beets well, and remove stem and tail ends. Cut into quarters, and chop them as fine as coleslaw. Mix with 2 quarts of water and bring to a rolling boil for 30 minutes. Replace any of the water which boils away. Set aside to cool to lukewarm.

Put the cut-up rhubarb into canner kettle and add remaining 2 quarts of cold water. When beets have cooled to lukewarm, strain juice from them into canner kettle. Squeeze pulp very dry, as you need every drop for coloring and flavor. Dissolve the sugar in 2 additional cups of water over a low flame. Dissolve to lukewarm, then add to beet-rhubarb mixture. Set in a warm place to ferment for two weeks. Stir and mash the rhubarb every day.

At the end of this two-week period, strain through jelly bag, squeezing very dry. Return liquid to canner kettle and add chopped raisins, ginger and peppercorns. Sprinkle the dry granulated yeast over the surface. Put in a warm place to ferment for three more weeks. Stir twice a week during this fermentation period.

After three weeks, strain again through jelly bag, and return to the canner kettle to settle for two days. Then siphon off into clean sterilized bottles and cork lightly. When there are no longer signs of fermentation, cork tightly and seal with paraffin. Keep for at least six months; however, a year's wait will reward your patience.

DARK RHUBARB WINE

4 quarts of rhubarb, cut into 1/2" pieces
4 quarts of cool water
8 cups of cane sugar
8 cups of black zante currants, finely chopped
1 package of dry granulated yeast (add after two weeks)

Soak currants overnight in 2 quarts of water. The next day, bring to a slow boil for 45 minutes, using the water in which they were soaked. Stir frequently to prevent scorching. Set aside to cool to lukewarm.

Then stir in the sugar, making sure it is all dissolved. Sprinkle package of dry yeast over the surface of the currants, and put in a warm place to ferment separately for two weeks. Stir every day.

Meanwhile put the cut-up rhubarb into canner kettle with remaining 2 quarts of water. Set in a warm place to ferment separately for two weeks. Stir every day, mashing and breaking up rhubarb as much as possible.

After two weeks, strain each of the mixtures and combine liquid from the two. Put this into canner kettle, and again put in a warm place for two more weeks of fermentation.

After this combined fermentation, strain through several thicknesses of cheesecloth, and siphon into clean sterilized bottles. Cork lightly until fermentation has ceased, and then cork tightly, sealing with paraffin. Keep for at least six months.

RHUBARB-FIG WINE

1st week:
4 quarts of rhubarb, cut into ½" pieces
2 lbs. of black figs, finely chopped
4 quarts of water
2nd week:
2 shredded wheat biscuits, *or* 1 cup of Wheat Chex
3rd week:
8 cups of cane sugar
1 package of dry granulated yeast

Combine cut-up rhubarb, chopped figs and water in canner kettle. Put in a warm place to ferment for one week. Then add crumbled shredded wheat biscuits or whole Wheat Chex. Put aside to ferment for one more week. During this entire two-week period, stir and crush the mash as often as possible every day.

At the end of this fermentation period, strain through jelly bag, squeezing pulp very dry. Return liquid to canner kettle, with the exception of 2 cups. Dissolve sugar in 2 cups of liquid over a low flame. While still hot, add to original rhubarb mixture. Sprinkle the dry granulated yeast over the surface and let stand two weeks longer. Stir twice a week during this fermentation period.

After two weeks, strain through several thicknesses of cheesecloth and siphon immediately into clean sterilized bottles. Cork lightly until fermentation has ceased; then cork tightly and seal with paraffin. Keep this wine for at least six months.

INDIAN RHUBARB WINE
(Sometimes called Corn Wine)

1st day:
4 quarts of rhubarb, cut into ½″ pieces
4 quarts of cool water
2nd day:
2 cups of cracked corn
Two weeks later:
8 cups of cane sugar
2 cups of muscat raisins, finely chopped
2 eggshells, finely crushed
1 package of dry granulated yeast

Put cut-up rhubarb into canner kettle with 4 quarts of water. Let stand overnight. The following day, stir in the cracked corn. Put in a warm place to ferment for two weeks. Stir every day during this time, crushing the rhubarb as much as possible each time you stir.

At the end of this two weeks of fermentation, strain through jelly bag, squeezing very dry. Return liquid to canner kettle. Stir in sugar, making sure that it is all dissolved. Add chopped raisins and finely crushed eggshells. Stir well again, and sprinkle the dry granulated yeast over the surface. Put in a warm place for three more weeks of fermentation. During this period a froth will rise to the top of the wine. This frothy material should be removed every day with a slotted spoon. At the end of this three weeks the froth will have diminished to practically nothing. If it is still present, let the wine stand until the froth disappears.

At that point you are ready to strain through cheesecloth and siphon into clean sterilized bottles. Cork this wine lightly at first, as it is very active in the bottle. At this stage it can be made into a sparkling wine which will effervesce when poured into the glass. The caution is: Use champagne bottles and long straight champagne corks if you want this. The corks must be fastened very tightly and secured with wire or heavy foil. Under no conditions attempt making this sparkling wine with ordinary bottles. The glass is far too thin and will not withstand the pressure. We tried it, and the explosions which resulted sounded as if we were testing atomic weapons at Yucca Flats. Not only that, but the mopping up was really something. To this day, if the light is right, you can see dainty crystals of broken glass driven into the ceiling of our wine cellar.

If I've frightened you away from the idea of a bubbling wine and you've decided to settle for the still variety, test each bottle by tapping for signs of bubbles running up the sides. If there are none, fermentation is over and it is safe to tighten the corks and seal with paraffin. Keep for at least six months, though it will be better after a year.

RHUBARB-AND-RED-RASPBERRY WINE

1st week:
- 2 quarts of "strawberry" rhubarb (this is the pink variety), cut into ½" pieces
- 2 quarts of red raspberries *or* 2 #2 cans of red raspberries
- 4 quarts of cool water

2nd stage:
- 8 cups of cane sugar
- 2 cups of white raisins, finely chopped
- 1 package of dry granulated yeast

Put the cut-up rhubarb into canner kettle; add water and well-crushed raspberries. Set in a warm place to ferment for one week. Stir every day, crushing the rhubarb against the sides of the canner kettle to break it up.

At the end of this week, strain through jelly bag, squeezing very dry to extract all liquid. Return liquid to canner kettle and add sugar, stirring well. When sugar is dissolved, add chopped raisins. Sprinkle dry yeast over the surface. Put in a warm place to ferment for two more weeks. Stir twice a week.

After this second two-week period, strain through several thicknesses of cheesecloth and return to the canner kettle to settle for two days more. Then siphon into clean sterilized bottles and cork lightly until fermentation has ceased. At that point, cork tightly and seal with paraffin. This wine should be kept for a year to mature properly.

RHUBARB-RASPBERRY-BLUEBERRY WINE

1st two weeks:
- 4 quarts of rhubarb, cut into ½" pieces
- 4 quarts of water

1 quart of red raspberries, *or* 2 #2 cans of red raspberries

1 quart of blueberries, *or* 2 #2 cans of blueberries

2nd two weeks:

8 cups of cane sugar

1 package of dry granulated yeast

Put the cut-up rhubarb into canner kettle with 2 quarts of water. In a separate kettle, crush raspberries and blueberries together and add remaining 2 quarts of water. Bring blueberries and raspberries to a boil for 30 minutes. Replace any water which boils away. If using canned fruit, add just as it comes from the can. Add the hot raspberry-blueberry mixture to the rhubarb and stir well. Put in a warm place to ferment for two weeks. Stir every day, crushing the rhubarb against the sides of the canner kettle to break it up.

At end of this two-week period, strain through jelly bag, squeezing very dry. Return liquid to canner kettle, with the exception of two cups. Dissolve sugar in the 2 cups of liquid, over a low flame. While still hot, add to original mixture. Sprinkle the dry yeast over the surface, and put in a warm place to ferment for two weeks longer.

Then strain through several thicknesses of cheesecloth, and siphon immediately into clean sterilized bottles. Cork lightly until fermentation has ceased, then cork tightly and seal with paraffin. Keep for six months.

RHUBARB-BOYSENBERRY WINE

1st two weeks:

4 quarts of rhubarb, cut into ½" pieces

4 quarts of water

3 #2 cans of boysenberries, sweetened or unsweetened

2nd two weeks:

8 cups of cane sugar

1 package of dry granulated yeast

Put the cut-up rhubarb into canner kettle and cover with 4 quarts of water. Stir in boysenberries—the syrup and fruit—just as they come from the can. If using fresh boysenberries, crush well with potato masher and add. Put in a warm place to ferment for two weeks. Every day during this time, stir and crush fruit against the sides of canner kettle.

At the end of this two-week period, strain through jelly

bag. Be very careful that no boysenberry seeds get into wine, as they impart an off taste and will make the wine cloudy. Return liquid to the canner kettle, except 2 cups. Dissolve sugar in the 2 cups of liquid over a low flame. While still hot, add to original mixture. Sprinkle the dry granulated yeast over the surface. Set in a warm place to ferment for two weeks longer.

Then strain through several thicknesses of cheesecloth and siphon immediately into clean sterilized bottles. Cork lightly until fermentation has ceased, then fasten the corks tightly and seal with paraffin. Keep for at least six months; if you can wait a year, you will have a much finer wine.

RHUBARB-PEACH WINE

1st two weeks:
  4 quarts of rhubarb, cut into 1/2" pieces
  4 quarts of water
  4 lbs. of dried peaches *or* 5 lbs. of fresh, quartered, unpeeled peaches
2nd two weeks:
  2 cups of muscat raisins, finely chopped
  8 cups of cane sugar
  1 package of dry granulated yeast

If you are using dried peaches, soak them overnight. The following day, bring them to a rapid boil for 30 minutes in the water in which they soaked. If using fresh peaches, chop them as fine as coleslaw.

Put the chopped or boiled peaches into canner kettle with the rhubarb and remainder of the water. Put in a warm place to ferment for two weeks. Stir every day, crushing fruit against sides of canner kettle to break it up.

After two weeks, strain through jelly bag, squeezing very dry. Return liquid to canner kettle, with the exception of 2 cups. Dissolve sugar in the 2 cups of liquid, over a low flame. While still hot, add to original mixture. Add raisins. Sprinkle dry granulated yeast over the surface, and set in a warm place to ferment for two more weeks.

Then strain through several thicknesses of cheesecloth, and siphon immediately into clean sterilized bottles. Cork lightly until fermentation has ceased, then cork tightly and seal with paraffin. Keep this wine for six months at least. Like all rhubarb wines, a year of aging really makes a wonderful wine.

RHUBARB-APRICOT WINE

1st two weeks:
4 quarts of rhubarb, cut into ½" pieces
4 quarts of cold water
2 lbs. of dried apricots
2nd two weeks:
2 cups of white raisins, finely chopped
8 cups of cane sugar
2 crushed eggshells
1 package of dry granulated yeast

Soak apricots overnight in 2 quarts of water. The next day, bring to a boil in same water for 30 minutes. Set aside to cool to lukewarm.

Put the cut-up rhubarb into canner kettle with 2 quarts of water. When the apricots have cooled, add to rhubarb. Set in a warm place to ferment for two weeks. Stir and break up fruit every day.

At the end of this two-week period, strain through jelly bag, squeezing the pulp very dry. Return liquid to canner kettle, with the exception of 2 cups. Dissolve sugar in the 2 cups of liquid, over a low flame. While still hot, add to original mixture. Also, add the raisins and crushed eggshell. Sprinkle the dry granulated yeast over the surface and put into a warm place to ferment for two weeks longer. Stir only twice a week during this time.

After this second two-week period, strain through several thicknesses of cheesecloth, and return to the canner kettle to settle for two days more. Then siphon into clean sterilized bottles and cork lightly. When fermentation has ceased, cork tightly and seal with paraffin. Keep for at least six months.

This is a light, wonderful wine to serve with fish and sea foods.

RHUBARB-STRAWBERRY WINE

1st two weeks:
4 quarts of pink "strawberry" rhubarb
4 quarts of fresh, very ripe strawberries
4 quarts of water

2nd two weeks:
  8 cups of cane sugar
  1 package of dry granulated yeast
Frozen strawberries may be used in this recipe; 6 commercial-sized packages will be needed. Thaw completely, and proceed as in the following recipe:

Put the cut-up rhubarb into canner kettle. In a separate bowl, crush the strawberries with potato masher until very fine. Add to the rhubarb with the water. Put in a warm place to ferment for two weeks. Stir daily.

At the end of this two-week period, strain through jelly bag, squeezing very dry. Return liquid to canner kettle and stir in the sugar, making sure it is all dissolved. Sprinkle the dry granulated yeast over the surface, and put in a warm place to ferment for two weeks more.

Then strain through several thicknesses of cheesecloth. If there are still strawberry seeds in the wine, strain again. Return liquid to canner kettle to settle for two days. Then siphon into clean sterilized bottles and cork lightly. When fermentation has stopped, cork tightly and seal with paraffin. Keep this wine for at least eight months. If your mother's strawberry-rhubarb conserve is a fond memory, this wine will make for some real nostalgia.

RHUBARB-PINEAPPLE WINE

1st two weeks:
  4 quarts of rhubarb, cut into 1/2" pieces
  4 quarts of water
2nd two weeks:
  2 fresh pineapples, ripened in the sun for several days, *or* 2 #2 cans of crushed pineapple
  8 cups of cane sugar
  2 cups of white raisins, finely chopped
  1 package of dry granulated yeast

Put the cut-up rhubarb into canner kettle and cover with 4 quarts of water. Set aside to ferment for two weeks. Stir daily, crushing rhubarb against sides of kettle to break up fruit.

Strain through jelly bag, squeezing well to extract all the liquid. Return to canner kettle and add the fresh pineapple —finely chopped—peelings and all, or the two cans of crushed pineapple, juice and all. Add the finely chopped raisins. Stir in sugar, making sure it is all dissolved. Sprinkle the dry granulated yeast over the surface. Put in a warm place to ferment for two more weeks.

Then strain through jelly bag, squeezing dry. Return to canner kettle to settle for two days more. Siphon into clean sterilized bottles and cork lightly. When fermentation has stopped, cork tightly and seal with paraffin. Keep this wine for at least six months.

RHUBARB-AND-RED-CHERRY WINE

1st two weeks:
4 quarts of "strawberry" rhubarb, cut into 1/2" pieces
3 quarts of tart red cherries
4 quarts of water
2nd two weeks:
8 cups of cane sugar
1 package of dry granulated yeast

Combine cut-up rhubarb and stemmed red cherries in canner kettle. Add 4 quarts of water, and put in a warm place to ferment for two weeks. Stir every day, crushing fruit against sides of canner kettle. Try to break up as many of the cherries as possible during this fermentation period, but be careful not to break open the cherry stones, as this will give a bitter taste to the wine.

At the end of this two-week period, strain through jelly bag, squeezing very dry. Return liquid to canner kettle and stir in the sugar, making sure all is dissolved. Sprinkle the dry granulated yeast over the surface, and set aside to ferment for two weeks longer. Stir only twice a week in this time.

After this second two weeks, strain through several thicknesses of cheesecloth, and return to canner kettle to settle for two days more. A deeper red may be given to this wine at this point by adding a teaspoon of red food coloring. When the wine has settled, siphon into clean sterilized bottles and cork lightly. When you are sure fermentation has ceased, cork tightly and seal with paraffin. Keep this wine for one year.

RHUBARB-PEACH-PLUM WINE

1st two weeks:
4 quarts of rhubarb, cut into ½″ pieces
4 quarts of Italian plums, halved and pitted
2 lbs. of dried peaches
4 quarts of tepid water
2nd two weeks:
8 cups of cane sugar
1 package of dry granulated yeast

In this recipe I have a preference for dried peaches instead of fresh. The dried fruit seems to give the wine a heavier body.

Put the cut-up rhubarb into canner kettle. Chop the plums very fine, and add them. Put the dried peaches through food chopper with the coarse blade and add, along with the 4 quarts of water. Put in a warm place to ferment for two weeks. Stir daily, mashing fruit against the sides of canner kettle.

After two weeks, strain through jelly bag, squeezing as dry as possible. Stir in the sugar and make absolutely sure it is all dissolved. Sprinkle dry granulated yeast over the surface and set in a warm place to ferment for two weeks more. Stir twice a week.

At the end of this second two-week period, strain through several thicknesses of cheesecloth, and return to the canner kettle once more to settle for two days. Siphon into clean sterilized bottles and cork lightly until fermentation has ceased. When fermentation is over, cork tightly and seal with paraffin. This is another wine that takes a year before it is ready to open, but you won't be sorry.

RHUBARB-AND-PRUNE WINE

1st two weeks:
4 quarts of rhubarb, cut into ½″ pieces
6 cups of prunes (soaked overnight in 2 quarts of water)
8 cups of cane sugar
2nd two weeks:
2 additional quarts of water
1 package of dry granulated yeast

After prunes have soaked overnight, bring to a boil in same

water for 30 minutes, or until the pits can be picked out easily with a fork. It is wise to remove the pits, for if any are broken in the wine it will have a bitter taste. Put the rhubarb into canner kettle and add remaining two quarts of water. Stir in prunes and their liquid. Put in a warm place to ferment for two weeks. Stir every day, mashing fruit against the sides of the canner kettle.

At the end of two weeks, strain through jelly bag, squeezing quite dry. Return liquid to canner kettle and add sugar, stirring very well so that all of it is dissolved. Sprinkle the dry granulated yeast over the surface. Put in a warm place to ferment for two weeks longer.

Then strain through several thicknesses of cheesecloth. Siphon immediately into clean sterilized bottles and cork lightly until all fermentation has ceased. Then cork tightly and seal with paraffin. Keep this wine for at least eight months.

CHAPTER X

From Vegetables Too?

When speaking of homemade wines, most people think only in terms of fruits and berries. However, there's quite a group of everyday root vegetables which can also be made into delicious wine.

The first time I ever heard of root vegetables being turned into wine was many years ago when my aunt began to tell my husband about the delicious carrot wine she had made. Since my spouse has always maintained that carrots are not fit food for humans and should be donated lavishly to the rabbit world, he immediately became interested.

Before the evening was over we had one canner kettle batch of wine started. It turned out to be very delicious and heavy-bodied. After six months it was a shade of topaz that was out of this world. To this day friend husband insists that this is the finest use to which he has ever seen the carrot put. From carrot wine we branched out experimentally into many of the other root vegetable wines, and they are still among our favorites.

CARROT WINE

4 lbs. of carrots (weight minus greens)
4 oranges cut into 1/4" slices
4 lemons cut into 1/4" slices
2 cups of muscat raisins, finely chopped
8 cups of cane sugar
12 peppercorns
1 ounce of wet yeast
1 slice of whole wheat toast

Scrub carrots well, but do not peel. Chop fine, or grate them as you would for a raw-carrot ring mould. Put carrots and water into canner kettle and bring to a rapid boil for 45 minutes. Set aside to cool to lukewarm.

Then strain through jelly bag, squeezing well to extract all liquid. Return to canner kettle and stir in the sugar, making sure it is all dissolved. Then add sliced oranges and lemons, and finely chopped raisins. Add the peppercorns if you desire a warm wine. Moisten the yeast with a few drops of water, and spread on one side of the whole wheat toast. Float the toast, yeast side down, on the surface of the liquid. Put in a warm place to ferment for two weeks. Stir every day during this two-week period.

Then strain again through jelly bag, squeezing very dry, and return to canner kettle to settle for two days longer. Siphon into clean sterilized bottles and cork lightly. When fermentation has stopped, seal tightly and dip in paraffin. Keep at least six months.

CARROT-PINEAPPLE WINE

4 lbs. of carrots
2 fresh pineapples, *or* 2 #2 cans of crushed pineapple
4 quarts of water
2 oranges cut into 1/4" slices
2 cups of muscat raisins, finely chopped
8 cups of cane sugar
8 peppercorns
1 ounce of wet yeast
1 slice of white toast

Scrub carrots well; then, without removing the peelings, chop very fine or grate. Put into canner kettle with the water and bring to a rapid boil for 45 minutes. Set aside to cool until lukewarm.

Be sure pineapples are very ripe. If they are not ripe enough to pull center spurs out easily, ripen in the open air on a sunny side of the house for several days. Do not remove the peelings; slice into 1/2" slices and chop as fine as coleslaw.

When carrot liquid has cooled to lukewarm, strain through jelly bag, squeezing very dry. Return to canner kettle and stir in sugar, making sure it is all dissolved. Then add the chopped pineapples. If using canned pineapple, put it in as it comes from the can, juice and all. Add oranges, chopped raisins and peppercorns. Moisten the yeast with a few drops of water and spread on one side of the toast. Float the toast, yeast side down, on the surface of liquid. Put in a warm place to ferment for two weeks. Stir every day during this time.

At the end of this two-week period, strain again through

128

jelly bag, squeezing very dry. Return liquid to canner kettle to settle for two days more. Then siphon off into clean sterilized bottles and cork lightly. When fermentation has ceased, cork tightly and seal with paraffin. Keep for six months.

CARROT-QUINCE WINE

    4 lbs. of carrots
    4 quarts of water
    10 large quince
    2 cups of black (zante) currants
    8 cups of cane sugar
    1 package of wet yeast
    1 slice of white toast

Scrub carrots well, but do not peel. Chop or grate very fine. Put into canner kettle with the water and boil for 45 minutes. Set aside to cool to lukewarm.

While this is cooling, quarter the quince, removing stem and seed portions. Chop up very fine. Put currants on to boil in two additional cups of water; boil for 30 minutes.

When carrot liquid has cooled to lukewarm, strain through jelly bag, squeezing very dry. Return liquid to canner kettle and stir in sugar. Add the finely chopped quince, and then add the boiled currants and their liquid while they are still hot. Moisten yeast with a few drops of water, and spread on one side of toast. Float the toast, yeast side down, on the surface of liquid. Put in a warm place to ferment for two weeks. Stir every day, inverting the quince which will rise to the top.

At the end of this two-week period, strain again through jelly bag, squeezing very dry. Return to canner kettle to settle for two days. Then siphon into clean sterilized bottles and cork lightly. When fermentation has ceased, cork tightly and seal with paraffin. Keep for at least six months.

CARROT-PRUNE WINE

    4 lbs. of carrots
    4 quarts of water
    2 lbs. of prunes
    1 cup of muscat raisins, finely chopped
    10 peppercorns

10 cassia buds
1 ounce of wet yeast
1 slice of whole wheat toast

Soak prunes overnight in 2 quarts of water. The next day, bring to a rapid boil in the same water. Boil 30 minutes, then set aside to cool.

Scrub carrots well, but do not peel. Chop or grate, and put on to boil for 45 minutes in the remaining 2 quarts of water. Set aside to cool to lukewarm.

Then strain through jelly bag, squeezing very dry. Return liquid to canner kettle and stir in sugar, making sure it is all dissolved. Add boiled prunes and water. Stir in the finely chopped raisins, add peppercorns and the cassia buds. Moisten the yeast with a few drops of water, and spread on one side of the toast. Float the toast, yeast side down, on the surface of the liquid. Put in a warm place to ferment for two weeks. Stir every day during this period.

After two weeks, strain again through jelly bag, squeezing quite dry. Return liquid to canner kettle to settle for two days longer. Then siphon into clean sterilized bottles and cork lightly until fermentation has ceased. When fermentation is over, cork tightly and seal with paraffin. Keep this wine for at least six months.

CARROT-APRICOT WINE

4 lbs. of carrots
4 quarts of water
3 lbs. of dried apricots (soaked overnight)
2 cups of muscat raisins, finely chopped
8 cups of cane sugar
1 ounce of wet yeast
1 slice of white toast

Soak apricots in 2 quarts of water overnight. The following day, bring to a boil for 30 minutes in same water. Stir frequently while they are boiling, so that they will not stick to the bottom and scorch. Set aside to cool.

Meanwhile, scrub carrots, but do not peel. Chop or grate fine and put into canner kettle with remaining 2 quarts of water. Boil for 45 minutes. Set aside to cool to lukewarm. When lukewarm, strain through jelly bag, squeezing very dry. Return liquid to canner kettle and stir in the sugar, making sure all is dissolved. Add finely chopped raisins and the apricots and their liquid. Moisten the yeast with a few drops of water and spread on one side of the toast. Float the toast, yeast side down, on surface of liquid. Put in a warm place to ferment for two weeks. Stir every day during this period, mashing well against the sides of the canner kettle.

After two weeks, strain through jelly bag, squeezing very dry. Return to canner kettle to settle for two days longer. Then siphon into clean sterilized bottles, corking lightly until fermentation has ceased. When fermentation is over, cork tightly and seal with paraffin. Keep for six months.

PLAIN RED BEET WINE

    5 lbs. of red beets
    4 quarts of water
    8 cups of sugar
    2 cups of cracked wheat
   10 peppercorns
    1 package of dry granulated yeast

Scrub the beets well, removing stems and tip ends, but do not peel. Chop very fine or grate; put into canner kettle with 4 quarts of water, and bring to a boil. Boil for 45 minutes, then set aside to cool.

When lukewarm, strain through jelly bag, squeezing very dry. Return liquid to canner kettle and stir in sugar, making sure all is dissolved. Stir in the cracked wheat and let stand for 15 minutes. Then stir again to break up any caking of the wheat. Add peppercorns. Sprinkle the dry granulated yeast over the surface and set in a warm place to ferment for two weeks. Stir every day during this fermentation.

Then strain through jelly bag, squeezing well. Return to canner kettle to settle for two days longer. Siphon off into clean sterilized bottles and cork lightly. When fermentation has ceased, cork tightly and seal with paraffin. Keep this wine for at least six months.

SPICED RED BEET WINE

    5 lbs. of red beets
    4 quarts of water
    8 cups of cane sugar
    4 lemons cut into 1/4" slices
   12 whole cloves

15 cassia buds
5 pieces of root ginger
10 peppercorns
1 package of dry granulated yeast

Scrub the beets well, removing the tip and stem, but do not peel. Chop very fine and put into canner kettle with the 4 quarts of water. Boil for 45 minutes and then set aside to cool to lukewarm.

When cool enough to handle, strain through jelly bag, squeezing well. Return liquid to canner kettle and stir in sugar, making sure it is all dissolved. Add sliced lemons, cloves, cassia buds, ginger and peppercorns. Sprinkle the dry granulated yeast over the surface, and then set in a warm place to ferment for two weeks. Stir every day.

At the end of this two-week period, strain again through several thicknesses of cheesecloth. Return to canner kettle to settle for two days. Then siphon into clean sterilized bottles and cork lightly. When fermentation has ceased, cork tightly and seal with paraffin. Keep for six months.

RED-BEET-AND-FIG WINE

5 lbs. of red beets
4 quarts of water
3 lbs. of dry black figs, finely chopped
8 cups of cane sugar *
juice of 3 lemons, *or* 1 small can of frozen lemonade
    concentrate
1 package of dry granulated yeast

Scrub the beets well, removing stem and tip ends. Chop very fine, and put into canner kettle with 4 quarts of water. Boil for 45 minutes. Set aside to cool.

When lukewarm, strain through jelly bag, squeezing well to extract all liquid. Stir in sugar, until all is dissolved. Add chopped black figs and lemon juice. Sprinkle the dry granulated yeast over the surface, then set in a warm place to ferment for two weeks. Stir well every day during this period.

At the end of two weeks, strain through jelly bag again, squeezing well to extract all of the liquid. Return to canner kettle to settle. If uncertain that all of the fig seeds were re-

---

* If using sweetened lemonade concentrate, diminish sugar by one cup.

moved in this last straining, strain through several thicknesses of cheesecloth before leaving to settle. Then siphon into clean sterilized bottles and cork lightly. When fermentation has ceased, cork tightly and seal with paraffin. Keep for six months.

RED-BEET-AND-RED-CURRANT WINE

1st week:
5 lbs. of red beets
3 quarts of ripe red currants
4 quarts of water
next step:
8 cups of cane sugar
1 package of dry granulated yeast

Scrub beets well, removing stem and tip ends. Chop very fine and put into canner kettle with 4 quarts of water. Bring to a boil for 45 minutes.

Meanwhile, pick over the currants, removing any stems. Do not wash, as that will remove natural wine yeast cells. Put into a large mixing bowl, and strain four cups of the boiling beet liquid into the currants. While still hot, crush gently with potato masher. This will set the color and release the flavor.

Strain the remainder of the beet mixture while still hot, and return liquid to canner kettle. Then add currant and beet-juice mixture. Set aside for one week, stirring every day and crushing currants against the sides of the canner kettle. After this week, strain through jelly bag, squeezing very dry. Return liquid to canner kettle and stir in the sugar, making sure it is all dissolved. Sprinkle the dry yeast over the surface and set in a warm place to ferment for two weeks. Do not disturb during this period.

After two weeks, strain through several thicknesses of cheesecloth. Siphon into clean sterilized bottles and cork lightly. When fermentation has ceased, cork tightly and seal with paraffin.

This is a wine that requires patience to the nth degree, for it must be kept at least eighteen months to gain its fullest body and flavor. I find the best system is to make it and then forget it. When you find it again eighteen months later, you'll never forget it again.

PLAIN POTATO WINE

Our name for this is "Poor Man's Rhine Wine," for after it is properly aged it's hard to tell from the real thing.

    3 lbs. of old potatoes (Idaho's are wonderful for this wine)
    2 cups of muscat raisins, finely chopped
    6 thin-skinned oranges, cut into 1/4" slices
    3 lemons cut into 1/4" slices
    8 cups of cane sugar
    4 quarts of water
    1 package of dry granulated yeast

Put water and sugar into canner kettle and set over a low flame. Stir until the sugar is dissolved, to prevent scorching.

While waiting for liquid to boil, scrub potatoes well, removing any eyes that may hold dirt. Slice about 1/4" thick—as for scalloped potatoes. Chop raisins and add to potatoes. Slice up oranges and lemons and add to potatoes.

When the sugar-water has reached the boiling stage, remove it from the stove. Stir in the mixture of potatoes, oranges, lemons, etc. Let cool to lukewarm, then sprinkle the dry granulated yeast over the surface. Put in a warm place to ferment for two weeks. Stir twice a week during this fermentation.

After two weeks, strain through jelly bag, and return liquid to canner kettle to settle for three days. Then siphon into clean sterilized bottles and cork lightly. When fermentation has ceased, cork tightly and seal with paraffin. Keep for at least six months.

SPICED POTATO WINE

    3 lbs. of old potatoes
    2 cups of muscat raisins, finely chopped
    8 cups of cane sugar
    2 cups of cracked wheat
    2 eggshells, finely crushed (add after two weeks)
    4 quarts of water
    1/4 lb. of candied ginger, finely chopped
    1 package of dry granulated yeast

Put sugar in a saucepan with 1 quart of water over a low

flame. Stir until the sugar is dissolved, to prevent scorching. Boil for 10 minutes.

Meanwhile, scrub the potatoes, removing all large deep eyes which may hold soil. Cut into 1/4" slices, but do not peel. Put potatoes into canner kettle with raisins and candied ginger and pour the boiling sugar-water over them. Add the remaining three quarts of water. Sprinkle in the cracked wheat. Let stand for 15 minutes, and then stir vigorously to break up any of the wheat which may have caked. Sprinkle the dry granulated yeast over the surface. Set in a warm place to ferment for two weeks. Stir daily to break up any of the wheat which may have formed lumps.

At the end of this two-week period, strain through jelly bag, extracting all of the liquid possible. Return liquid to canner kettle and sprinkle in crushed eggshells. Let stand for one more week.

Then strain through several thicknesses of cheesecloth. Immediately siphon into clean sterilized bottles and cork lightly. When fermentation has ceased, cork tightly and seal with paraffin. Keep for at least six months.

Parsnips

Parsnips have been called the poor man's vegetable, but I personally don't know of any vegetable that is such an un-favorite among any people, rich or poor. Creamed, fried, or boiled, they are just hard to put over. Seldom do you see them on a restaurant menu. However, if you have just planted your north eighty acres under parsnips, take heart, for you can make wine out of them—delicious wine at that!

PLAIN PARSNIP WINE

   6 lbs. of parsnips
   4 quarts of water
   8 cups of cane sugar
   2 cups of white raisins, finely chopped
   1 slice of white toast
   1 ounce of wet yeast

Use young parsnips, for if they are tough old boys, they will be bitter. Scrub well, getting all the soil from the ridges; do not peel. Chop fine or grate and put into canner kettle with 4 quarts of water. Cook for 45 minutes, uncovered. Set aside to cool to lukewarm.

Then strain through jelly bag, squeezing lightly so that no pulp is forced through into the wine; this would cause cloudiness. Return liquid to canner kettle and stir in sugar until all is dissolved. Add the chopped raisins. When liquid is lukewarm, moisten the yeast and spread on the toast. Float the toast, yeast side down, on the surface of the liquid. Put in a warm place to ferment for two weeks, stirring twice a week.

After two weeks, strain again through jelly bag. Return to canner kettle and let settle for two days more. Then siphon off into clean sterilized bottles and cork lightly. When fermentation has ceased, cork tightly and seal with paraffin. Keep for at least six months.

PARSNIP-AND-PRUNE WINE

    6 lbs of parsnips
    2 lbs. of prunes
    4 quarts of water
    8 cups of cane sugar
    1 slice of whole wheat toast
    1 ounce of wet yeast

Soak prunes overnight in 2 quarts of water. The next day bring to a slow boil in the same water for 30 minutes.

Meanwhile, scrub parsnips well, removing all signs of soil. Chop or grate into canner kettle. Add 2 quarts of water and bring to a slow boil for 45 minutes. Set both the prune and the parsnip mixture aside to cool to lukewarm.

When parsnips are cool, strain through jelly bag, and return liquid to canner kettle. Add the cooled prunes, liquid and all. Stir in sugar, making sure it is all dissolved. Moisten the yeast with a few drops of water, and spread on the whole wheat toast, and float toast, yeast side down on the surface of the lukewarm liquid. Set in a warm place to ferment for two weeks. Stir every day, breaking and crushing the prunes as much as possible during this time.

After two weeks, strain through jelly bag and return to canner kettle to settle for two days more. Siphon into clean sterilized bottles and cork lightly. When fermentation is over, cork tightly and seal with paraffin. Keep for at least eight months. This is a sweet, heavy wine with a unique flavor—an excellent dessert wine.

PARSNIP-AND-PEACH WINE

6 lbs. of parsnips
4 lbs. of fresh peaches
4 quarts of water
8 cups of cane sugar
12 peppercorns
12 cassia buds
1 slice of whole wheat toast
1 ounce of wet yeast

Scrub parsnips very well, removing stem ends; then chop very fine. Put into canner kettle with 4 quarts of water and boil for 45 minutes, uncovered. Let cool. Meanwhile, quarter peaches and remove stones. Chop very fine.

When parsnips are cool enough to handle, strain through jelly bag. Return liquid to canner kettle and stir in the sugar, making sure it is all dissolved. Add chopped peaches, cassia buds and peppercorns. Moisten the yeast with a few drops of water and spread on one side of the toast. Float the toast, yeast side down, on the surface of the liquid. Put in a warm place to ferment for two weeks. Stir daily, mashing the fruit against sides of canner kettle.

At end of this two-week period, strain through jelly bag, squeezing very dry. Return to canner kettle to settle for two days more. Siphon into clean sterilized bottles, corking lightly. Watch this wine carefully during the fermentation period in the bottle, as it is very active. Be sure fermentation is over before corking tightly and sealing with paraffin. Keep for six months.

PARSNIP-AND-LEMON WINE

4 lbs. of parsnips
12 large clear-skinned lemons, cut in ¼" slices
4 quarts of water
8 cups of cane sugar
2 cups of white raisins, finely chopped
1 slice of white toast
1 ounce of wet yeast

Scrub the parsnips very well to remove soil. Cut off tip ends and chop very fine. Put into canner kettle with 4 quarts of water; bring to a boil for 45 minutes. Set aside to cool to lukewarm.

When lukewarm, strain through jelly bag, squeezing gently. Return liquid to canner kettle and stir in the sugar until all is dissolved. Add chopped raisins and sliced lemons. Moisten the yeast with a few drops of water and spread on one side of the toast. When liquid is lukewarm, float the toast, yeast side down, on the surface of the liquid. Set in a warm place to ferment for two weeks. Stir daily during this time.

At the end of two weeks, strain through jelly bag, squeezing gently, so that no bitter taste from the white part of the lemon is squeezed into the wine. Return to canner kettle to settle for two days more. Then siphon off into clean sterilized bottles and cork lightly. When fermentation has ceased, cork tightly and seal with paraffin. Keep for at least six months. If you prefer a drier wine, diminish the sugar by half.

PARSNIP-AND-GINGER WINE

5 lbs. of parsnips
¼ lb. of candied ginger, finely chopped
2 cups of white raisins, finely chopped
4 quarts of water
8 cups of cane sugar
12 peppercorns
1 slice of white toast
1 ounce of wet yeast

Scrub parsnips well, removing stem ends. Chop or grate very fine and put into canner kettle with 4 quarts of water. Leave uncovered and boil for 45 minutes. Set aside to cool to lukewarm.

Then strain through jelly bag, squeezing gently. Return to canner kettle and stir in sugar, until all is dissolved. Add chopped raisins, ginger and peppercorns. Moisten the yeast with a few drops of water, and spread on one side of the toast. Float the toast, yeast side down, on the surface of the liquid. Put in a warm place to ferment for two weeks. Stir every day (from the bottom, to keep the piece of toast intact as long as possible).

After two weeks, strain through jelly bag. Immediately siphon into clean sterilized bottles and cork lightly. When all signs of fermentation have ceased, cork tightly and seal with paraffin. Keep for at least six months. If kept a year, this wine will develop a very pleasant spicy flavor and a deep color. It lends itself well to warming winter wine drinks.

PARSNIP-AND-QUINCE WINE

5 lbs. of parsnips
3 lbs. of fresh quince
4 quarts of water
3 lemons cut into 1/4″ slices
8 cups of cane sugar
2 cups of white raisins, finely chopped
1 slice of white toast
1 ounce of wet yeast

Scrub parsnips well and remove stem ends. Chop or grate quite fine and put into canner kettle with 4 quarts of water. Peel quince thoroughly. Quarter and remove seed pockets; then chop or grate fine. Add quince to parsnips and water, and bring to a boil for 45 minutes. Set aside to cool to lukewarm.

Then strain through jelly bag, squeezing out as much liquid as possible. Return to canner kettle and stir in the sugar until completely dissolved. Add chopped raisins and sliced lemons. Moisten yeast with a few drops of water, and spread on one side of the toast. Float the toast, yeast side down, on the surface of the liquid. Put in a warm place to ferment for two weeks. Stir gently twice a week, keeping the toast intact.

After two weeks, strain through jelly bag, and return liquid to canner kettle to settle for two days longer. Siphon into clean sterilized bottles and cork lightly. When fermentation has ceased, cork tightly and seal with paraffin. To have a really excellent wine, keep for at least nine months.

PARSNIP-AND-RED-BEET WINE

5 lbs. of parsnips
3 lbs. of red beets
1 #2 can of tart pie cherries
2 cups of muscat raisins, finely chopped
8 cups of cane sugar
1 slice of whole wheat toast
1 ounce of wet yeast

Scrub parsnips well, and remove stem ends. Grate or chop

very fine and put into canner kettle. Scrub the beets well, but do not peel. Remove stem ends, and grate or chop very fine, and add to parsnips, together with 4 quarts of water; boil for 45 minutes. Set aside to cool.

When lukewarm, strain through jelly bag, squeezing well. Return liquid to canner kettle and stir in the sugar, making sure all is dissolved. Add can of cherries, juice and all, and the finely chopped raisins. Stir well until thoroughly mixed. Moisten yeast with a few drops of water and spread on one side of the toast. Float the toast, yeast side down, on the surface of the liquid. Set in a warm place to ferment for two weeks. Stir gently twice a week.

After two weeks, strain through jelly bag, squeezing quite dry. Return to the canner kettle to settle for two days more. Then siphon into clean sterilized bottles and cork lightly. When fermentation has stopped, cork tightly and seal with paraffin. Keep for six months.

Anise Root

Midsummer finds anise roots on display at the markets. This beautiful celerylike plant is a delicacy in Italy and the south of France. In this country perhaps children know its flavor best; it tastes like licorice. However, if you've never tried fresh anise root, slip some into your next tossed salad; it is delicate and delicious. It comes in large bundles—the stalks are sometimes a foot in length. The root is topped with the beautiful, green, lacy foliage and whenever I buy it I always use the tips with garden flowers as a centerpiece for the table. The leaves have a languid appearance, and there's something in the way they hang that is reminiscent of Spanish moss. Anise Root Wine has a flavor like absinthe, with none of the evil effects.

ANISE ROOT WINE

    2 good-sized anise roots
    4 quarts of water
    6 cups of cane sugar
    2 cups of white raisins, finely chopped
    1 ounce of wet yeast
    1 slice of white toast
Remove the green foliage quite far down the stalk; then

separate the anise root and scrub well to remove all soil. Cut into 1/2" pieces and put into canner kettle along with 4 quarts of water. Bring to a boil and boil for 35 minutes. Set aside to cool to lukewarm.

Then strain through jelly bag, squeezing well to remove all liquid. Add the sugar, stirring well to dissolve completely. Stir in chopped raisins. Moisten yeast with a few drops of water and spread on one side of the toast. Float the toast, yeast side down, on the surface of liquid. Set in a warm place to ferment for two weeks. Stir very gently every day during this time.

After two weeks, strain through several thicknesses of cheesecloth and return to the canner kettle to settle for two days longer. Then siphon off into clean sterilized bottles and cork lightly. When fermentation has stopped, cork tightly and seal with paraffin. Keep for eight months.

CELERY WINE

4 stalks of bleached or green celery
8 cups of cane sugar
4 quarts of water
1 ounce of wet yeast
1 slice of white toast

Scrub celery well with a brush to remove black soil between ridges. Remove all foliage. Cut into 1/2" pieces and put in canner kettle with 4 quarts of water. Bring to a boil for 45 minutes. Set aside to cool to lukewarm.

Then strain through jelly bag, squeezing well to extract all liquid. Stir in sugar, making sure all is dissolved. Moisten the yeast with a few drops of water and spread on one side of the toast. Float the toast, yeast side down, on the surface of the liquid. Set in a warm place to ferment for two weeks.

At the end of this period, strain through several thicknesses of cheesecloth and return to the canner kettle to settle for two days. Then siphon off into clean sterilized bottles and cork lightly. When fermentation has ceased, cork tightly and seal with paraffin. Keep for eight months. This is a surprisingly delicious wine.

TURNIP WINE

Mammy Yokum and her "presarved turnip" routine had

me mystified for years. Personally, I couldn't see why anyone would save a turnip, much less preserve one. Now I think I know. Last year I made just a half gallon of turnip wine. This year I intend to make much more.

4 quarts of chopped turnips (approximately 8 lbs.)
8 cups of cane sugar
3 quarts of water
Add after one week:
10 peppercorns
1 cup of domestic brandy

Peel turnips. Cut into chunks and then chop very fine with chopping knife. Put into canner kettle. Dissolve sugar in 3 quarts of water over a low flame. While still warm, pour over chopped turnips. Set in a warm place to ferment for one week.

Then strain through jelly bag, squeezing as dry as possible. Return juice to canner kettle and add the cup of brandy and the peppercorns. Set in a warm place to ferment for two weeks more.

At the end of this period, strain through several thicknesses of cheesecloth. Siphon into clean sterilized bottles and cork lightly until fermentation has ceased; then cork tightly and seal with paraffin. Keep for six months.

TOMATO WINE

Here's a good use for those surplus tomatoes.

4 quarts of sliced, unpeeled tomatoes
4 quarts of water
8 cups of cane sugar
1 tablespoon of salt
¼ lb. of candied ginger, finely chopped
1 ounce of wet yeast
1 slice of white toast

Slice the unpeeled tomatoes, and sprinkle tablespoon of salt over them. Meanwhile, combine the sugar and water in canner kettle and bring to a rapid boil for 15 minutes. Remove from the stove, and immediately put in sliced tomatoes and finely chopped ginger. Stir well and set aside to cool to lukewarm.

Then moisten the yeast with a little water and spread on

one side of the toast; float the toast, yeast side down, on surface of liquid. Put in a warm place to ferment for two weeks. Stir every day, breaking up the tomato slices as much as possible during the stirring.

After two weeks, strain through jelly bag, squeezing well to extract all of the liquid. Return to the canner kettle to settle for one week longer. Then siphon off into clean sterilized bottles and cork very lightly.

This wine should stand with loosened corks for at least two weeks. Check carefully for signs of fermentation, for this wine has explosive tendencies if corked too soon. When there are no further signs of fermentation, cork tightly and seal with paraffin. Keep for at least three months, though six months of aging makes it much better.

CHAPTER XI

Wine from Citrus Fruits and Flowers

There was a time in America when an orange was considered a very special and expensive treat. Giving a six-week-old baby orange juice was unheard of by our ancestors. However, a Christmas stocking without an orange to fill out the toe just wasn't according to tradition.

Today oranges, lemons, grapefruit and limes are as necessary a part of our diet as milk. Thanks to our marvelous shipping industry, citrus fruits are enjoyed by all at any time at very reasonable prices. The citrus fruit wines which follow are an excellent addition to any meal, and go well with all foods.

(The recipes for wines from the blossoms of citrus fruits are included in this chapter because they are so regionally limited.)

ORANGE WINE

1st day:
3 dozen clear-skinned oranges
6 cups of cane sugar
2 quarts of water
1 egg white (save the shell)
2nd day:
1 ounce of wet yeast
1 slice of white toast
1 cup of grape brandy (optional) (add after two weeks)

Peel oranges and save peelings in a separate large mixing bowl. Avoid getting too much white with the peelings, but peel as thin as possible. Halve oranges and squeeze the juice from them. Strain juice through a coarse sieve to remove seeds. Put juice into a two-quart fruit jar; let stand at room temperature overnight.

Then combine sugar, white of egg and 2 quarts of water in a pan and put over a low flame to boil. Boil until egg white froth is floating on surface of water. While still boiling hot, strain through a fine sieve into the bowl containing orange peel. Let this stand overnight also.

The following day, combine in canner kettle orange juice and water in which the peelings soaked. Throw away the peelings; if they were put into the mash they would make the wine bitter. Moisten yeast with a few drops of water and spread on one side of the toast. Float the toast, yeast side down, on surface of liquid. Put in a warm place to ferment for two weeks without disturbing.

Then strain through several thicknesses of cheesecloth and return to the canner kettle. Sprinkle crushed eggshell over the surface and let stand for two days longer. Then siphon into clean sterilized bottles. When siphoning, take care not to get the siphon on the bottom of the kettle, for this will draw up the settled material. An inch from the bottom the wine becomes cloudy. Stop siphoning, and put remainder in a large glass jar to settle a little longer.

Seal by corking lightly at first, and when there are no more signs of fermentation, cork tightly and seal with paraffin. Keep this wine for at least nine months.

The optional cup of brandy can be added at the same time as the crushed eggshell—that is, before the two-day settling period. This addition of brandy will heighten the alcohol volume and give the wine added warmth. For further information on fortification of wine see the chapter "The Spirit Is Willing If—."

ORANGE BLOSSOM WINE

Orange blossoms at weddings used to be the real thing, but now they are seldom seen—which makes me wonder if all the blossoms are being converted into wine. Here is the recipe:

- 4 quarts of orange blossoms, picked when the dew is off, and then dried in the sun for several hours. (Be sure to remove the green end.)
- 4 quarts of water
- 8 cups of cane sugar
- 3 oranges, sliced ¼" thick
- 2 cups of white raisins, finely chopped
- 1 package of dry granulated yeast

Pour the water over the orange blossoms and simmer

145

slowly for 20 minutes. Strain carefully and put aside to cool.

When lukewarm, stir in the sugar until thoroughly dissolved. Add sliced oranges and chopped raisins. Sprinkle dry granulated yeast over the surface and set in a warm place to ferment for two weeks. Stir daily.

At the end of this two-week period, strain through jelly bag, squeezing well. Return liquid to canner kettle to settle for one more week. Then siphon into clean sterilized bottles and cork lightly. When fermentation has definitely ceased, cork tightly and seal with paraffin. Keep for at least three months, though six months will greatly improve the wine.

LEMON WINE

24 clear-skinned lemons and peelings
4 quarts of boiling water
8 cups of cane sugar
1 egg white (save the shell)
2 cups of cracked wheat
1 cup of muscat raisins, finely chopped
1 package of dry granulated yeast

Peel lemons, keeping peelings as thin as possible, avoiding the white material underneath. Put peelings in large mixing bowl. Combine sugar, water, white of egg and crushed eggshell in a saucepan. Put over low heat, and stir until sugar is all dissolved. Bring to a boil, and boil until froth of egg white is floating on the surface. Then strain into bowl containing lemon peelings. Let stand overnight at room temperature.

Next day, squeeze the lemons and strain juice through a coarse sieve; discard seeds. Put juice and sugar-water in which peelings soaked into canner kettle. (Throw away the peelings.) Stir in chopped raisins and cracked wheat. Let settle for 15 minutes, then stir again to break up any caked wheat. Sprinkle dry granulated yeast over the surface and put in a warm place to ferment for two weeks. Stir every day during this period.

After two weeks, strain through jelly bag, squeezing very dry. Return to canner kettle to settle for one week more. Siphon off into clean sterilized bottles and cork lightly. When fermentation has ceased, cork tightly and seal with paraffin. Keep this wine for nine months.

SPICED ORANGE-AND-LEMON CHRISTMAS WINE

8 oranges cut into 1/4" slices
6 lemons cut into 1/4" slices
1/4 lb. of candied ginger, finely chopped
1 ounce of whole cloves
2 cups of white raisins, finely chopped
12 peppercorns
1 slice of white toast
1 ounce of wet yeast
4 quarts of water
8 cups sugar

Put sliced oranges and lemons into canner kettle. Add candied ginger and raisins. Add 3 quarts of water with peppercorns and cloves.

Dissolve sugar in remaining quart of water over a low flame. While still hot, stir into spice-and-fruit mixture. Moisten yeast with a few drops of water, and spread on one side of the toast. Float toast, yeast side down, on surface of liquid. Set in a warm place to ferment for two weeks. Stir every day during this fermentation.

After two weeks, strain through jelly bag, squeezing lightly. Return liquid to canner kettle for one more week of fermentation. Then strain through several thicknesses of cheesecloth and return to the canner kettle to settle for two days. Siphon into clean sterilized bottles and cork lightly until fermentation has ceased. When it is definitely over, cork bottle tightly and seal with paraffin. Keep for at least three months before using. We call this Christmas wine because, if made in September when oranges are plentiful, it will be ready —and just right—at Christmastime.

GRAPEFRUIT WINE

4 quarts of fresh grapefruit juice (half pink meat is excellent)
6 cups of cane sugar
2 lemons cut into 1/4" slices
8 peppercorns
1 package of dry granulated yeast

This wine is best made in a glass container, such as a gallon-sized wide-mouthed jar. Squeeze juice from grapefruit. Strain to avoid seeds and white membrane, which impart bitterness.

Dissolve sugar in 2 cups of the grapefruit juice over a low flame. While still hot, pour into original juice. Add sliced lemons and peppercorns. This makes more than a gallon of juice; reserve balance in a clean sterilized lightly corked bottle to fill the jars as the wine works over the top. Sprinkle dry granulated yeast over the surface and cover with ordinary table saucers, bottom side down, so that the wine is free to work out from under them. Set in a warm place to ferment for three weeks. Stir twice a week.

At the end of this three-week period, siphon off carefully into another clean gallon jar, avoiding any settlings at bottom of original jar. Let ferment for one week longer.

Then siphon into clean sterilized bottles, corking lightly. When fermentation is over, cork tightly and seal with paraffin. Keep for six months.

LIME WINE

    2 dozen juicy limes
    4 quarts of water
    8 cups of cane sugar
    2 cups of white raisins, finely chopped
    1 slice of white toast
    1 ounce of wet yeast

Peel limes and reserve peelings in a large mixing bowl. Combine the sugar with 2 quarts of water and bring to a boil for 15 minutes. Pour boiling sugar-water over peelings and let stand overnight.

The following day, squeeze the juice from limes and put into canner kettle with the 2 remaining quarts of water. Add chopped raisins. Then strain into canner kettle the sugar-water which soaked the lime peelings. (Throw away the peelings.) Moisten the yeast with a few drops of water, and spread on one side of toast. Float toast, yeast side down, on the surface of the liquid. Put in a warm place to ferment for two weeks.

Then strain through jelly bag, squeezing very dry. Return liquid to canner kettle to settle for one additional week. Then siphon into clean sterilized bottles and cork lightly. When fermentation has ceased, cork tightly and seal with paraffin.

Keep for at least four months. Served over crushed ice, this wine makes an excellent summer drink.

LIME BLOSSOM WINE

4 quarts of lime blossoms (Dry in the sun for several hours and be sure that there is no green material left on them.)
4 quarts of water
6 cups of cane sugar
1 cup of white raisins, finely chopped
1 package of dry granulated yeast
2 limes cut in 1/4" slices (lemons may be substituted)

Combine water and flowers in canner kettle and simmer for 30 minutes. Remove from fire and, when cool enough to handle, strain through jelly bag, squeezing well.

Return liquid to canner kettle and stir in sugar until dissolved. Add the limes or lemons and the chopped raisins. When liquid has cooled to lukewarm, sprinkle the dry granulated yeast over the surface. Set in a warm place to ferment for two weeks.

Then strain through several thicknesses of cheesecloth, and return to canner kettle to settle for one week more. After that time, siphon off into clean sterilized bottles and cork lightly. When fermentation has ceased, cork tightly and seal with paraffin. Keep this wine at least three months—six, if you have the patience.

TANGERINE WINE

24 clear-skinned tangerines
3 quarts of water
6 cups of cane sugar
1 egg white (save the shell)
1 ounce of wet yeast
1 slice of white toast

Peel tangerines as you would for eating. Tear peelings in pieces the size of a quarter. Eliminate the white center stem membrane. Put torn peelings into large mixing bowl.

Combine sugar, water, and the white of egg in a saucepan. Place over a low flame and boil until the egg white rises to the surface in froth. Strain hot sugar-water over tangerine peelings. Let stand overnight.

The following day, put tangerine pulp into canner kettle and mash well with potato masher. Strain peelings from sugar-water, throw the peelings away and add the sugar-water to the mashed tangerines. Set aside to ferment for one week.

Then strain through jelly bag, squeezing very dry. Return liquid to canner kettle. Moisten the yeast with a few drops of water and spread on one side of toast. Float the toast, yeast side down, on surface of liquid. Set in a warm place to ferment for one more week.

After this second week, sprinkle in crushed eggshell, and continue fermenting for one week more. (Shell acts as a clearing agent.)

Then strain through several thicknesses of cheesecloth, and return to canner kettle to settle for two more days. Then siphon into clean sterilized bottles and cork lightly. When fermentation is over, cork tightly and seal with paraffin. Keep for six months.

TANGERINE BLOSSOM WINE

    4 quarts of tangerine blossoms (Dry in the sun for several
      hours; remove green material.)
    4 quarts of water
    6 cups of cane sugar
    1 cup of white raisins, finely chopped
    2 lemons cut in ¼″ slices
    1 package of dry granulated yeast

Combine flowers and water in canner kettle and bring to a simmer for 30 minutes. Remove from the fire and let cool to lukewarm.

Then strain through jelly bag, squeezing very well. Add sugar, stirring until all is dissolved. Add raisins and sliced lemons. When mixture is not too hot, sprinkle in dry granulated yeast. Put in a warm place to ferment for two weeks. Stir daily.

After two weeks, strain through jelly bag again, squeezing very dry. Return to canner kettle to settle for two days more.

Then siphon off into clean sterilized bottles, corking lightly until all fermentation has stopped. When wine is no longer working, fasten corks tightly and seal with paraffin. Keep for at least six months.

CHAPTER XII

Wine from Grains

As mentioned earlier, making wine from grains goes back to the Romans. In fact, during Cicero's time, there was a prohibition against grape growing north of the Alps and many of the grain wine recipes still in use today originated there.

All these wines require grain in its dried natural state. Obtaining these grains, untampered with by tenderizing or pearling, is not always easy. I have had my best luck at health food stores, and have also bought grain directly from farmers. The search for raw materials for grain wines is worth it in fine flavor.

BARLEY WINE

- 2 cups of natural barley (Do *not* use the popular pearled barley made for soup.)
- 2 cups of white raisins, finely chopped
- 8 cups of cane sugar
- 3 Idaho potatoes, scrubbed but not peeled
- 4 quarts of tepid water
- 1 package of dry granulated yeast

Slice potatoes as you would for scalloped potatoes, but do not peel. Put into canner kettle with raisins, barley and sugar. Add 4 quarts of tepid water, and stir until all sugar is dissolved. Then sprinkle the dry granulated yeast over the surface. Put in a warm place to ferment for two weeks. Stir every day, pushing down mash which rises to the top.

After two weeks, strain through jelly bag and return liquid to canner kettle to settle for one additional week. At the end of this time (this makes three weeks in all), siphon off into clean sterilized bottles and cork very lightly.

Watch this wine closely during the fermentation in the bottle; do not cork it tightly too soon. But when you are sure fermentation is over, then cork tightly and seal with paraffin. Keep for six months; a year's wait is truly rewarding.

CORN WINE

2 lbs. of cracked corn (buy at feed store, or dry your own and put through food grinder)

1st day:
3 oranges, and peelings
3 lemons, and peelings
2 cups of muscat raisins, finely chopped
3 quarts of water

2nd day:
8 cups of cane sugar
1 quart of water
1 package of dry granulated yeast
12 peppercorns

Peel oranges and lemons. Reserve peelings in canner kettle. Add cracked corn, chopped raisins and 3 quarts of the water. Let stand in a warm place overnight.

The following day, dissolve sugar in remaining quart of water over a low flame. Squeeze oranges and lemons peeled the previous day, and strain juice into corn mixture. Stir sugar-water, while still warm, into corn mixture, mixing well so that sugar is evenly distributed. Sprinkle dry granulated yeast over surface. Put in warm place to ferment for two weeks. Stir every day during this time.

After two weeks, strain through jelly bag, squeezing gently. Return liquid to canner kettle for one week more. Then strain through several thicknesses of cheesecloth, and return to the canner kettle for another two days of settling. Siphon into clean sterilized bottles and cork very, very lightly—set corks in the necks of the bottles without any pressure whatever. This wine does a great deal of fermenting in the bottle, and if corked too tightly during this time it may explode. Watch closely for about six weeks, and if after that time there is no fermentation going on, fasten the corks tightly and seal with paraffin. A good test is to tap each bottle, and if there are no bubbles running up the side, fermentation is over. This wine should be kept for at least six months.

Corn wine adapts itself well to a warming agent. If you like the warm sensation in wine, add 12 peppercorns, at the same time that you sprinkle in the dry granulated yeast.

GOLDEN WHEAT WINE

1st day:
6 cups of cracked wheat
4 quarts of water
2 cups of white raisins, finely chopped
2nd day:
8 cups of cane sugar
1 package of dry granulated yeast

Preheat oven to 375° F. Spread wheat on two shallow baking pans. Watch it carefully. When top surface of wheat begins to brown, turn over with a wide spatula. Continue turning until it is all the same golden brown. Then remove from oven and set aside to cool.

When cool, put wheat into canner kettle with raisins and water. Set in a warm place overnight.

The following day, stir in sugar until thoroughly dissolved. Sprinkle the dry granulated yeast over the surface. Put in a warm place to ferment for two weeks. Stir daily during this time.

After two weeks, strain through jelly bag, squeezing well. Return liquid to canner kettle to settle for one week more. At the end of this week (this is three weeks in all), siphon into clean sterilized bottles. Cork very lightly for the first two weeks of bottle fermentation. When fermentation has stopped, cork tightly and seal with paraffin. Keep for at least three months.

HEAVY WHEAT WINE

3 cups of cracked wheat
3 cups of muscat raisins, finely chopped
2 cups of prunes (soak overnight in one quart of water)
3 large Idaho potatoes, unpeeled
8 cups of sugar
1 orange cut into 1/4" slices
1 lemon cut into 1/4" slices
3 additional quarts of water
1 package of dry granulated yeast

Soak prunes overnight in 1 quart of water. The following day simmer for 30 minutes, or until the fruit separates from the stones. While still hot, stir in sugar until completely dissolved.

Scrub potatoes well and slice as you would for scalloped potatoes. Put into canner kettle with chopped raisins, sliced lemons and oranges. Add 3 remaining quarts of water, and stir in prunes, juice, and cracked whole wheat. Stir all very well and let settle for 15 minutes, then stir again to break up any wheat lumps. Sprinkle the dry granulated yeast over the surface and put in a warm place to ferment for two weeks. Stir every day during this fermentation.

After two weeks, strain through jelly bag and return to canner kettle for one more week. Then strain through several thicknesses of cheesecloth, and siphon into clean sterilized bottles. Cork lightly for the first week, or until fermentation has stopped. Then cork tightly and seal with paraffin. Keep for at least four months, though longer aging really improves this wine.

RICE WINE (Sake)

- 6 cups of unpolished rice (available at health food stores)
- 2 cups of white raisins, finely chopped
- 6 cups of cane sugar
- 4 quarts of water
- 1 package of dry granulated yeast
- 1 crushed eggshell (used in the final week of fermentation)

Combine rice and raisins in canner kettle with 2 quarts of the water. Dissolve sugar in remaining 2 quarts over a low flame. While still hot, stir into rice-raisin mixture. Let cool to lukewarm, and sprinkle the dry granulated yeast over surface. Set in a warm place to ferment for two weeks. Stir every day from the bottom to prevent rice forming into lumps.

After two weeks, strain through jelly bag and return liquid to canner kettle for an additional week of fermentation. Sprinkle crushed eggshell over surface of liquid at this time. This will settle and clear the wine. Siphon into clean sterilized bottles at the end of this week, keeping hose from bottom of kettle. Cork wine lightly until fermentation is definitely over; then cork tightly and seal with paraffin. Keep for six months at least; however, a year's aging really makes this wine worthy of old Nippon.

RYE WINE

4 cups of rye grain
8 cups of cane sugar
4 quarts of tepid water
2 Idaho potatoes, unpeeled
2 clear-skinned lemons, cut into ¼″ slices
1 package of dry granulated yeast

Scrub potatoes and remove eyes which may hold soil. Cut into convenient chunks for chopping. Chop as fine as coleslaw. Put potatoes, sliced lemons and rye into canner kettle. Add 2 quarts of water. Dissolve sugar in remaining 2 quarts over a low flame. While still hot, stir into rye mixture. Sprinkle dry granulated yeast over the surface and put into a warm place to ferment for two weeks. Stir twice a week.

Then strain through jelly bag and return liquid to canner kettle to settle for two days more. Then siphon off into clean sterilized bottles. Cork very lightly at first—set cork into mouth of bottle, using no pressure whatever. When fermentation is definitely over, cork tightly and seal with paraffin. Keep for at least six months.

Rye wine is a Swedish favorite; it is sometimes made from coarsely ground rye, too, but we found that the coarsely ground rye made the wine take longer to clear in the final stages.

CHAPTER XIII

Meads, or Wines Made with Honey

Mead is perhaps the oldest known form of wine. All through mythology, mead is mentioned as a favorite beverage of the gods.

Odin, the chief of Norse gods, was very fond of mead. As he sat on his cloudy throne ruling the universe, two wolves, Geri and Freki, lounged at his feet. Odin gave them all the meat set before him, for, being a god, he had no need of mere food. Mead was for him both food and drink. Odin didn't come by his favorite beverage honestly, however. He stole it from a giant called Suptung after a fierce duel. Mead served the ancient poets, too. It was supposed to be a source of inspiration. Whether planning to dash off a quatrain or not, you should try making mead—it is delicious and different. Honey is used as the main fermenting agent.

BRIGHT RED CURRANT MEAD

1 5-lb. pail of honey
4 quarts of red currants
4 quarts of water
2 cups of muscat raisins, finely chopped
1 ounce of wet yeast
1 slice of white toast

Combine honey and water in canner kettle and bring to a rolling boil for 10 minutes. Skim off any froth rising to the surface.

Meanwhile, crush currants until all are broken. Remove honey-water from stove, and immediately stir in crushed currants. Then set aside to cool to lukewarm.

When lukewarm, add finely chopped raisins, stirring well so that they are evenly distributed. Moisten yeast with a few drops of water and spread on one side of the toast. Float the toast, yeast side down, on surface of liquid. Put in a warm place to ferment for two weeks.

Then strain through jelly bag, squeezing very dry to extract all of the juice. Return to canner kettle to ferment for two weeks more.

At the end of this second fermenting period, strain through several thicknesses of cheesecloth and immediately siphon into clean sterilized bottles. Cork lightly. When fermentation has stopped, cork tightly and seal with paraffin. Keep for at least six months.

Bright Red Mead is wonderful served over chipped ice as a summer drink. It can also be served with sparkling water or sweet soda and ice.

DEEP RED RASPBERRY MEAD

1 5-lb. pail of honey
4 quarts of black raspberries, tame or wild
2 quarts of red raspberries, tame or wild
4 quarts of water
2 cups of muscat raisins, finely chopped
1 ounce of wet yeast
1 slice of white toast

Combine water and honey in canner kettle and bring to a rolling boil for 10 minutes. Skim off froth rising to surface. Meanwhile, combine black and red raspberries and crush very fine with potato masher. Remove honey-water from stove and immediately stir in crushed berries. Set aside to cool to lukewarm.

Then stir in raisins. Moisten yeast with a few drops of water and spread on one side of toast. Float the toast, yeast side down, on the surface of the liquid. Set in a warm place to ferment for two weeks.

At the end of this time, strain through jelly bag, squeezing very dry. Return liquid to canner kettle for two more weeks of fermentation.

Then strain through several thicknesses of cheesecloth to catch any remaining raspberry seeds and further clear wine. Siphon immediately into clean sterilized bottles and cork lightly until fermentation has stopped. When fermentation is over, cork tightly and seal with paraffin. Keep for six months.

SPICED MEAD

1 5-lb. pail of honey

4 quarts of water
¼ lb. of candied ginger, finely chopped
3 tablespoons of whole cloves
3 tablespoons of mace
3 tablespoons of cassia buds
1 package of dry granulated yeast

Combine water and honey in canner kettle and bring to a rolling boil for 10 minutes. Skim off froth rising to surface. Put cloves, mace and cassia buds into small muslin bag, and drop into liquid during the last 5 minutes of boiling. Remove from stove and add finely chopped candied ginger. Set aside to cool to lukewarm. Leave all spices in mead during first fermentation.

When lukewarm, sprinkle the dry granulated yeast over the surface and put in a warm place to ferment for two weeks. No stirring is necessary.

After two weeks, strain through several thicknesses of cheesecloth, and return liquid to canner kettle to settle for one week. Then siphon into clean sterilized bottles and cork lightly. When all fermentation has stopped, cork tightly and seal with paraffin. Keep this wine for at least three months.

Spiced Mead is a favorite of the Scandinavians, and it is often served warm as a winter drink.

STRAWBERRY MEAD

We call this "Pink Ambrosia" for it tastes like the essence of everything good in the world.

4 quarts of very ripe strawberries
1 5-lb. pail of honey
1 #2 can of crushed pineapple
4 quarts of water
2 cups of white raisins, finely chopped
1 package of dry granulated yeast

Combine water and honey in canner kettle and bring to a rolling boil for 10 minutes. Skim off any rising froth. Meanwhile, crush strawberries very fine with potato masher. Remove the honey-water from stove and immediately stir in strawberries. Set aside to cool to lukewarm.

Then stir in crushed pineapple and chopped raisins. Sprinkle dry granulated yeast over surface and put in a warm place to ferment for two weeks. Stir daily.

After two weeks, strain through jelly bag, squeezing very dry. Return to canner kettle to settle for two days more. Then siphon off into clean sterilized bottles and cork lightly. When fermentation has stopped, cork tightly and seal with paraffin. Keep this wine for at least eight months. A year's aging produces a special treat.

GOLDEN PINEAPPLE MEAD

If you've ever tasted really ripe pineapple right out of the field—you've lived. The little green knobs which find their way to market are like taking apples off the trees in June—some flavor is there, but it seems just a promise of things to come. So it is with pineapple in its "fresh state," as we get it. There is a solution. Buy green pineapples and set them outside for a week in the direct sun, turning a different side to the sun every day. The trouble and patience involved are worth it. I, for one, will never again slice a pineapple just as it came from the store.

After ripening pineapple in this manner, consult the following recipe for making one of the most wonderful meads in the world. (While this book was being written, there was talk of field-ripened pineapple being shipped in frozen. That would be wonderful, but I haven't been able to find any as yet.)

2 large ripened pineapples
4 quarts of water
1 5-lb. pail of honey
2 cups of white raisins, finely chopped
1 package of dry granulated yeast

Combine water and honey in canner kettle; bring to a rolling boil for 10 minutes. Skim off any surface froth. Meanwhile, cut pineapple into convenient pieces for chopping, but do not peel. Chop pineapple as fine as coleslaw. Remove the honey-water from stove and immediately stir in chopped pineapples. Set aside to cool to lukewarm.

Then stir in finely chopped raisins, and sprinkle dry granulated yeast over the surface. Set in a warm place to ferment for two weeks. Stir every day in this time.

After two weeks, strain through jelly bag, squeezing very dry. Return liquid to canner kettle to settle for two days. Even after this the wine will retain a cloudiness, but it will disappear in the bottling. Siphon into clean sterilized bottles after settling period, and cork lightly. When fermentation has definitely ceased, cork tightly and seal with paraffin. Keep for six months.

Golden Mead makes a wonderful after-dinner dessert wine. It is excellent if added to salad dressings, and a chilled fruit cup with a jigger of Golden Mead added is an Olympian pleasure.

TOPAZ OR RAISIN MEAD

6 cups of seedless raisins, finely chopped
1 5-lb. pail of honey
4 quarts of water
2 oranges cut into 1/4" slices
2 lemons cut into 1/4" slices
1 ounce of wet yeast
1 slice of whole wheat toast

Combine water and honey in canner kettle and bring to a rolling boil for 10 minutes. Skim off surface froth. Set aside to cool to lukewarm.

Then stir in raisins, sliced lemons and oranges. Moisten the yeast with a few drops of water and spread on one side of the toast. Float the toast, yeast side down, on the surface of liquid. Put in a warm place to ferment for three weeks. Stir daily.

After three weeks, strain through jelly bag, squeezing very dry. Return to canner kettle to settle for two days more. Then siphon off into clean sterilized bottles and cork lightly. When fermentation has stopped, cork tightly and seal with paraffin. Keep for four months. Aging longer will make a much clearer wine, and the body will be heavier, too.

GOOSEBERRY MEAD

4 quarts of gooseberries (on the green side)
1 5-lb. pail of honey
4 quarts of water
2 cups of light raisins, finely chopped
1 package of dry granulated yeast

Combine water and honey in canner kettle and bring to a rolling boil for 10 minutes. Skim off surface froth. Let cool to lukewarm.

Meanwhile, crush gooseberries very fine with potato masher. When the honey-water mixture has cooled, add crushed gooseberries and finely chopped raisins. Sprinkle dry granulated yeast over the surface and put in a warm place to ferment for two weeks. Stir and invert the mash daily.

At the end of this two-week period, strain through jelly bag, squeezing very dry. Return liquid to canner kettle to settle for two days more. Then siphon into clean sterilized bottles and cork lightly. When fermentation has ceased, cork tightly and seal with paraffin. Keep for six months.

DANDELION MEAD

4 quarts of dandelion blossoms (See direction under "Wine from Flower Petals" for cleaning the dandelions and avoiding bitterness in wine.)
1 5-lb. pail of honey
4 quarts of water
2 lemons cut into $\frac{1}{4}$" slices
1 package of dry granulated yeast

Combine water and honey in canner kettle and bring to a rolling boil for 10 minutes. Skim off froth. Put sliced lemons in a separate bowl and cover with 2 cups of the boiling liquid. Set lemons aside until the next day.

Remove honey-water mixture from stove and stir in the cleaned dandelion blossoms. Put aside until the next day. The following day, add the lemons and their liquid. Then sprinkle dry granulated yeast on surface and allow to stand for one week. Strain through jelly bag, squeezing very dry. Return liquid to canner kettle for one more week of fermentation.

Then strain through several thicknesses of cheesecloth and siphon immediately into clean sterilized bottles. Cork lightly until fermentation has definitely ceased; then cork tightly and seal with paraffin. Keep for at least six months.

COWSLIP MEAD

6 quarts of cowslip blossoms (For cleaning, etc., see directions in "Wine from Flower Petals.")
4 quarts of water
1 5-lb. pail of honey
2 lemons cut into $\frac{1}{4}$" slices

2 oranges cut into ¼″ slices
1 package of dry granulated yeast

Combine water and honey in canner kettle and bring to rolling boil for 10 minutes. Skim off froth on surface. Put sliced lemons and oranges in a bowl; cover with 3 cups of the boiling liquid; set aside until the next day. While honey-water mixture is still hot, stir in the cowslip blossoms and set this aside too until the next day.

The following day, add oranges, lemons and their liquid to the blossom mixture. Let stand for three days. Then strain through jelly bag, squeezing very dry. Return liquid to canner kettle and let settle for one week longer.

Then siphon into clean sterilized bottles and cork very lightly until fermentation is definitely over. Before corking tightly, tap each bottle for bubbles up the sides. When you are sure wine is through fermenting, cork tightly and seal with paraffin.

This wine has a very delicate, appealing flavor, and is a lovely shade of yellow-green in the glass.

CHAPTER XIV

And That Reminds Me. . . .

There are literally thousands of ways to make homemade wines. The differences between recipes exist only in the quantities and number of ingredients used, and the manner in which they are added to the first mash. I mention this because at some time or other someone will say, "Is that how *you* do it? Now, my grandfather always used to put. . . ." Whether Granddad dropped raisins in the mash one at a time, or chopped them fine, will make little difference in the end product. By adding all fruits chopped fine, as I have advised, only one thing occurs—fermentation.

There are hundreds of regional fruits and berries which have not been covered by this book. If there is a wonderful fruit or edible berry growing in your locality which should make good wine, just follow the recipe for the fruit or berry it most closely resembles.

Flowers, fruits, and berries grow pretty much alike the world over. By following the seed structure of any fruit, a comparable fruit can be found. Seeds grow either internally or externally. Melons are perhaps the best example of internal seed growth; here, the outer covering (not the skin, but the meat) which we know as the edible part, acts as a protector and a nutrient for the young seeds inside. Strawberries and raspberries, on the other hand, are perhaps the most common examples of outer seed growth; here the edible parts acts as a cushion and nutrient to the young seeds. Apples, pears, peaches and plums fall into the same structural class as melons, for their seeds are protected by a layer of material which is edible.

After deciding the seed classification of an unlisted fruit and choosing a recipe in the book, observe all of the things regarding yeast cells on the skin, natural sugars, coloring ability, etc., pointed out at the beginning of each chapter.

Experimenting with different fruits is fun—especially if they grow in great abundance near where you live. When making flower wines, compare the texture of the blossoms, then follow a similar flower recipe.

How to Build a Wine Stock

With today's high cost of mere existence, few households boast more than two or three different kinds of wine for table use or entertainment purposes. Then, too, the variety of inexpensive commercial wines is limited to four or five kinds. However, a little time and effort and a pair of wide-open eyes for bargains are the only requirements (except money) for building a wine stock which will meet the requirements of any occasion, or go with any meal.

Here's the easy way: Say you happen to pick up this book in the dead of winter and the only things showing on trees are Christmas lights. Fine. Start with a gallon of Grapefruit Wine, for when Christmas bills run high, grapefruit are in season and low in price. As soon as the grapefruit wine is at the clearing stage, Spiced Orange-and-Lemon Christmas Wine can be started. Then, too, tangerines are very cheap, so a gallon of Tangerine Wine is in order. And since raisins are always on the grocers' shelves at reasonable prices, a supply of Nippy Light Raisin Wine could be made. Before you know it, you will have four gallons—sixteen quarts—of wine aging for your pleasure.

Mapping out a program of winemaking—devoting just one month to one wine—will result in twelve gallons, or ninety-six quarts, at the year's end. Bottle by bottle, a wine cellar can be built that will afford countless hours of pleasure. Federal law permits the making of two hundred gallons per year—and a gallon a month wouldn't even put a dent in this allowance. And the few hours you steal from some other task to make the wine will never be missed.

When my husband and I first started our winemaking, we laid down a rule for this wine-of-the-month routine. One month we would make a heavy sweet wine, the following month a light dry wine. In this way we could serve all tastes. Alternating from dry to sweet wines means a well-rounded stock from which to choose. It's gratifying to cope with the somebody who says, after one taste, "Oh, this is nice, but a little too dry for me . . ." by instantly producing a sweet wine for him.

Perhaps the most important thing in making wine by the

164

gallon-a-month method is labeling. I mentioned earlier in the book my fondness for Mystik Tape. To be able to go into my wine cellar and put my hands on properly labeled bottles is wonderful. No holding up to the light wondering, or opening the wrong bottle by mistake. Mystik Tape sticks and stays; it retains its markings year in and year out. Memory plays tricks on the best of us; I have been guilty of putting bottles of wine into the cellar without labeling when time was scarce, only to find that I couldn't remember, a month later, what was in them. When the wine is in dark glass bottles, holding them up to the light is like trying to pick out a new dress while wearing sunglasses. I keep my supply of Mystik Tape right in the wine cellar now, along with a good ballpoint pen, and by guess and by gosh have gone out of my life forever.

Storing Wine

I know I've spoken casually of a wine cellar—it just so happens that we have a house with one. To be faced with no cellar, just kitchen storage space, doesn't mean all is lost. While aging, wine can be stored in the back of an infrequently used cupboard, if it is not too warm, and if the bottles are covered with several layers of brown paper to keep light out.

A quiet corner of a basement can make a good wine cellar. It needs no windows, for light is no friend of wine.

If the job of constructing racks to hold the bottles is an unhappy prospect for your husband, an old cupboard or a set of pre-fab basement shelves will serve just as well. In fact, orange crates or apple boxes can be turned into wonderful wine storage space. All that is needed is a piece of board nailed across the front of the box to hold the bottles at a tilt. Wooden blocks, or just crumbled newspaper stuffed at the back, will hold the bottles approximately at a 22-degree angle.

One more note on basements for storing wine—they are a natural. The guide at Mammoth Cave in Kentucky astounded me with the fact that the temperature of the earth immediately below the frostline is always 56°. For some reason or other, wines that are stored in the bottle enjoy any temperature in the fifties, so a basement is a logical storing place for the products of the home winemaker.

I have paid close attention to the temperatures in my own

basement. In the wine cellar, which is shut away from the heating plant, the temperature seldom gets out of the 50-degree range. Most basements have higher humidity than the rest of a house, and this is a help, too, in keeping bottle corks from becoming dry and brittle.

A cork can be trusted for about a year in a wine bottle standing upright. But even in a year's time a certain amount of evaporation will take place, and the wine will no longer be touching the cork. When wine is being aged longer than a year, it must be tilted so that the wine is against the cork at all times. Corks have a nasty habit of shrinking and reducing with age. Even properly tilted bottles should be inspected from time to time to see whether they are holding their own.

Sadly, too, the variety of cork on the market today is not so solid and close as it was years ago. If a cork has many brown markings, do not trust it more than a year. Nice solid corks are wonderful, but rather hard to find.

Despite the paraffin seal, described earlier in the book, corks sometimes will cry musty tears, and the paraffin will bulge and become discolored. This is a sure sign that the wine must be used immediately, or rebottled and resealed.

This inspection of wine bottles is really no task at all for me. From time to time I find myself proudly mulling over this wine or that. It's more or less like a bottled diary—every wine brings nostalgic memories of the day I picked the blossoms, or the night I was all set to put it through the jelly bag and the Smiths dropped in. . . .

Blending Wines

Blending wines is an old practice. Among European wine-makers, a wine blender is high paid and greatly revered. The opening of the wine casks for testing and blending has always been an occasion of much anticipation and ceremony.

After each sample of wine, the "official tester" takes a piece of dark rye bread sprinkled with salt and chews it well to erase from his taste buds the wine sampled before. These men test wines that have been aging in the casks for years, and the welfare of the whole community depends upon their judgment. It is easy to understand why such great importance is attached to the opening of the casks, and why excitement runs so high.

After the wine has been tested and graded, blending is considered. Blending of wines in most European wineries is only a matter of good budgeting. When a wine region has a good grape year, followed by one in which the grapes are small and dwarfed upon the vine, there is nothing to do but blend. (The prospect of eating chicken one year and just the feathers the next is dismal.) So the wine of the good grape year is blended with the mediocre wine of the bad year. A passably good product in both years is the result of this blending.

However, all the wine of the good year is not used to bring the poorer wine up to standard. Perhaps only 20% is used this way; 80% is retained for distribution as a high-grade product.

The blending of homemade wines is not a matter of higher economics, but purely of taste. If, when having a glass of Elderberry Flower Wine, the thought occurs, "Hmmm . . . now if this just had a little of the headiness of that Dandelion Wine I made. . . ." go ahead and combine the two. Of course, it's best to experiment with small quantities. When you've found just the proportions you like, then mix the whole bottleful. Then recork and reseal just as you did when the wine was first made. Give the two wines at least three months to get thoroughly acquainted in the bottle before opening it again.

When blending wine, flowers do not have to be combined with flowers or fruits with fruits. Flower wine can be blended with berry wine; root vegetable wine can be blended with berry, and some pretty wondrous things will result! Just give that imagination and those unbridled taste buds a chance to work, and then start blending!

The contents of your wine cellar can be multiplied, as far as variety is concerned, if you combine some of the wine. When blending wines, don't forget to label the bottles, because it is very easy to end up with a "delicious mystery wine" for which you lost the combination.

Blending for the home winemaker is a timesaver, too. Mixing the finished wine, rather than raw materials, avoids the mess of keeping a dual mash. And the element of risk is practically nil; you are mixing two agreeable flavors when they are at the peak of perfection!

Choosing the Right Wine

Choosing the proper wine for the proper food is a subject for countless books. This advice, however, is devoted purely to wine proper, "the fermented juice of the grape."

The home winemaker, with ingredients other than grapes, has to serve his wines more or less by rule of thumb. There is just one question to ask yourself: Does the wine complement the food? Do they go together, match each other, like the new hat you bought to go with that pinkish stripe in your new blouse? It's as simple as that. When serving a beef roast, resplendent with heavy gravy, naturally a wine which is not too rich in body should be served. Or pick one of the innumerable dry red wines. If serving a dainty luncheon of salad and handcarved melon balls, choose sweet light wine. Here again, kaleidoscopic imagination and uninhibited taste buds should be allowed to guide you.

When mentioning wine with meals, most people have a pregrade-school attitude, as if they were blending colors— they insist that the kindergarten teacher pointed out that purple and green don't go together. So it is with wines. Years back, hard and fast rules were set down: Red wines go with red meats and white wines go with fish and similar foods. This is fine for grapes, but the rule melts away with homemade wines—then imagination is required!

Every good hostess knows that you should not try out new dishes on guests; so it is with wines. Test the wine with the food you intend to serve. If the flavors do not argue with each other—serve them. Always sneak a taste of the combination first.

Making Passes at Glasses

There was a time when the subject of the proper glass for the proper wine could either make or break a lady socially. Shades of the bustle! If a Gay Nineties hostess had mistakenly served a medium sherry in a cuplike Rhine glass, she had had it.

Thank goodness that, by popular demand, the glass manufacturers of this country have come down to earth. They still manufacture sherries, Rhines, hollow-stems, etc., but they have helped solve the problem of which glass to use by making many types which are suitable for serving a variety of drinks—from dry Martinis to sherry.

In the bad old days a properly equipped china closet had to contain twenty-four sherry glasses, twenty-four Rhine wines, twenty-four liqueurs, twenty-four hollow-stems, twenty-four shallow champagnes, and so on, until the money ran out. Of course, that was in the day, too, when a strong girl with a weak mind was hired for three dollars a week to do almost nothing but wash all these glasses.

The American glass companies have put their prices within reach, too. For less than half a dollar each, I have bought wine glasses which were beauties to behold. Too, when the tragedy of breaking takes place, there is no great loss. Eight glasses today can be bought for the price of one of Grandmother's rock-crystal Rhine goblets. Until you've inherited a set of hand-cut wine glasses, one of which was accidently tipped and broken, minor tragedy hasn't struck. The top shelf of the cupboard is where most reasonable people keep the hand-cut stuff; as far as I'm concerned that's where it should stay. Elegant wine service is beautiful but difficult and, most of the time, impossible to replace.

American hot-cast wine glasses can look almost as beautiful on your table as cut crystal. There is only one rule: Before pouring wine, be sure the glasses are buffed to their sparkling best and reflect every light in the room.

As Your Pour

During the settling period mentioned in most of the recipes, some solids will stay on the bottom of the canner kettle, and will cause you no trouble if you take care not to let them get into the bottle. However, sometimes a cloudy condition remains in the bottle in spite of all your efforts. Eventually this will clear and settle on the bottom of the bottle and, of course, you do not want to rouse this up into the wine again. Avoid any vigorous action between storage place and place of serving.

We have always repoured our wine from its storage bottle into a decanter. There are many advantages in this. First and foremost, the wine can be poured off without any settlings. This settling is not limited to homemade wines, by the way, for I have read innumerable books on European wines and their serving, and they all advise the use of a decanter.

In fact, most of these books suggest "giving the last glass of wine to the bottle."

If, at any time, settlings have inadvertently been stirred up in a bottle of wine, and there is no time for resettling, use an ordinary funnel for pouring wine from the bottle into the decanter. Then put a wad of sterile cotton into the bottom of the funnel just above the funnel opening, and pour the wine. It will come through into the decanter as clear as the crystal from which you will drink it.

Using a decanter for serving is also wise since most wine bottles are stored undisturbed and collect a certain amount of dust. By the time the dust is wiped off the wine will be all stirred up. However, if you can ease the wine into the decanter from the dusty bottle, there will be no need for wiping the bottle, and the wine will be ready and beautiful to serve.

Keeping wine calm before serving is of utmost importance. When bringing wine from its storage place to where it is to be served, avoid any vigorous action. A good policy is to handle it as if it were a grenade; then you will have only clear wine in your glasses.

Uncle Sam says....

In addition to the requirement regarding federal wine permits, there is another federal ruling governing wine. Under no conditions send wine or other alcohol through the United States mails.

Uncle Sam doesn't care if it *is* your Uncle Louie's hundredth birthday—wine and alcohol are just not mail travelers. The express companies, too, are not permitted to carry alcohol over state lines.

This is it! Here end all afterthoughts of homemade wines.

Remember, wine is the only beverage that improves in the bottle. Most wine will be full and ripe at the end of six months, and a delight at the end of a year.

Since every one of us comes into this world with a built-in imagination and a good stock of patience—the two most important ingredients for making your own wines—I know you'll have no end of luck and pleasure!

INDEX

171

174

IF YOU ENJOYED THIS BOOK
YOU WILL ALSO WANT TO READ

Mettja C. Roate's

THE NEW HAMBURGER COOKBOOK

The homemaker learns how to use hamburger in 365 different ways—in casseroles, meat loaves, cookout treats, pizzas, even soup. There's enough variety to fit any mood or occasion—enough taste satisfaction to make eating a pleasure for months to come.

75-155　　　　　　　　　　　　　　　　　　**75¢**

COOKING WITH CHEESE

Add zing to soups, breads and cocktail dips with cheese recipes as easy as they are delicious. Here are endless ways to use cheese in sandwiches, fondues, main dishes and vegetables. Add the good taste of cheese to your daily diet, every day of the year.

75174　　　　　　　　　　　　　　　　　　**75¢**

COOKING WITH CHICKEN

Tired of chicken always tasting the same? Here are nearly 200 ways this appetite-pleaser can rejuvenate your meals, in everything from standard favorites to way-out gourmet dishes for special occasions. Whether you're a beginner or an expert, you'll find both inspiration and satisfaction in this unique collection.

75-178　　　　　　　　　　　　　　　　　　**75¢**

All books available at your local newsdealer. If he cannot supply you, order direct from Macfadden-Bartell Corporation, 205 East 42nd Street, New York, New York, 10017. Enclose price listed for each book, plus 10¢ extra per book to cover cost of wrapping and mailing.